Crosscurrents / Modern Critiques / New Series

Edited by Harry T. Moore and Matthew J. Bruccoli

James Gould Cozzens: New Acquist of True Experience
Edited by Matthew J. Bruccoli

Thomas Pynchon: The Art of Allusion
By David Cowart

Twentieth-Century American Literary Naturalism: An Interpretation
By Donald Pizer

Twentieth-Century American Literary Naturalism

An Interpretation

By Donald Pizer

Southern Illinois University Press

Carbondale and Edwardsville

Copyright © 1982 by Southern Illinois University Press
Printed in the United States of America
Edited by Daniel M. Finnegan
Designed by Gary Gore
Production supervised by Richard Neal

Library of Congress Cataloging in Publication Data,

Pizer, Donald.
   Twentieth-century American literary naturalism.

   (Crosscurrents/modern critiques. New series)
   Bibliography: p.
   Includes index.
   1. American fiction—20th century—History and criticism.
2. Naturalism in literature. I. Title.
II. Series.
PS374.N29P5   813'.5'0912   81–5606
ISBN 0–8093–1027–9   AACR2

For Margaret

Contents

Preface

Conclusion

An important paradox characterizes the history of American literary naturalism. Although the movement has been attacked by literary journalists and academic critics since its origin in the 1890s, it has been one of the most persistent and vital strains in American fiction. As Willard Thorp noted in 1960, naturalism "refuses to die" in America despite the deep antagonism it usually inspires.[1] Few of our major twentieth-century novelists have escaped its "taint," and it is perhaps the only modern literary form in America which has been both popular and significant.

There are a number of reasons for the opposition to naturalism.[2] Because much naturalism is sordid and sensational in subject matter, it is often dismissed out of hand by moralists and religionists. The early naturalists were particularly vulnerable in this regard. A more meaningful antagonism arises from the feeling of many readers of naturalistic fiction that their basic assumptions about human nature and experience are being challenged. Man's faith in his innate moral sense and thus his responsibility for his actions, and his belief in the semi-divine nature of the American experience and in the healing and preserving roles of family and love—these and many other traditional values appear to be under attack in the naturalistic novel. Many readers have also objected to the fullness of social documentation in most naturalistic fiction. From the early attack on naturalism as "mere photography" to the recent call for a fiction of "fabulation," the aesthetic validity of the naturalistic novel has often been questioned.

These traditional objections to naturalism arise for the most part from a priori beliefs about man and fiction. The most probing critics of naturalism have attacked it not on these grounds but on those implied by the ideological origins of the movement. They have argued that a fiction as ideological as naturalism should have a unified and coherent philosophical base and a distinctive form and style consistent with that base. This position has its origin, whether acknowledged or not, in the preeminence of Zola's theory of literary naturalism, and in particular in Zola's belief that the

ix

naturalist is a scientist manqué who describes human behavior as closely related to the demonstrable material factors which have conditioned it. Naturalism, in this still widespread view, is above all social realism laced with the idea of determinism.[3] We live in a biologically and socially conditioned world, and it is the function of the novelist to demonstrate this truth. An entire generation of critics has argued, however, that naturalists have been hopelessly confused because they introduce elements of free will and moral responsibility into accounts of a supposedly necessitarian world.[4] Even Charles Walcutt, who avoids the trap of condemning naturalists for their allegiance to two seemingly irreconcilable systems of value (the "two streams" of his major study of naturalism in America),[5] nevertheless slips into the related position of faulting the movement for not producing distinctive literary forms consistent with its deterministic philosophy. No wonder, then, that naturalism in America has always been in ill repute. Whether damned for degrading man beyond recognition by depicting him as a creature at the mercy of "forces" ("Not Men," in Malcolm Cowley's well-known phrase)[6] or attacked for inconsistency because of the presence of characteristics which fail to debase him, the naturalist has seldom lacked detractors.

Yet despite this unceasing and almost unanimous assault on almost every aspect of American naturalism, the movement, unlike its European counterpart, has continued to flourish. A number of reasons have been advanced to explain the hold of naturalism upon both our writers and our readers. Because of its documentary method, the naturalistic novel, it is argued, has a concreteness and circumstantiality particularly congenial to the American temperament. Alfred Kazin sums up this notion when he writes that "with us naturalism has been not so much a school as a climate of feeling, almost in the very air of our modern American life, with its mass patterns, its rapid social changes, its idolatry of the mechanical and of 'facts.'"[7] Naturalistic fiction is not only "familiar" in its solidity but is also, unlike much modern fiction, fully and strongly plotted. From *McTeague* to *Lie Down in Darkness*, the narrative as "story" is a powerful characteristic of the naturalistic novel even when it contains various experimental techniques. Naturalistic fiction also attracts many readers (while repelling others) because of its sensationalism. "Terrible things must happen to the characters of the naturalistic tale," Frank Norris wrote in 1896,[8] and so it has been ever since. The sensationalism of naturalistic fiction, however—its violence and sexuality, for example—has an appeal which strikes deeper than the popular taste for the prurient and titilating. The extraordinariness of character and event in the naturalistic novel creates a potential for symbolism and allegory, since the combination of the concrete and the exceptional immediately implies meanings beyond the surface. Naturalism is thus closely related to the romance in its reliance on a sensationalistic symbolism and allegory. And if, as Richard Chase and others have argued,[9] the romance—as in the fiction of Hawthorne and Melville—is the form most native to the distinctive American experience, then naturalism is a form which continues to fulfill this need in American life.

These explanations of the sources of appeal of naturalism in America—its closeness to many of the requirements of popular taste yet the implication of a deeper level of attraction as well—have prompted my own method in this study. My approach has not been the conventional one of beginning with a definition of naturalism derived from late nineteenth-century ideas and conditions and then judging writers in accordance with their degree of conformity to the definition. It is this critical procedure, as I have suggested, which has contributed to the misunderstanding of and hostility toward the movement. Because I have sought rather to write an empirical account of naturalism in America, I have begun with a loose sense or impression of what constitutes a naturalistic novel, an impression gathered largely from my earlier examination of American naturalistic fiction of the 1890s. After selecting a number of major novels which appear to bear a resemblance to this impression, I have attempted out of a close reading of these novels to derive a number of general ideas about naturalism in America without a commitment to the discovery of a single, static definition. I have, in brief, written a book about naturalism in which a detailed study of potentially naturalistic novels suggests that there is no neat definition applicable to the movement in America but rather a variable and changing and complex set of assumptions about man and fiction which can be called a naturalistic tradition.

The working hypothesis which guided my selection of novels for further consideration is that naturalistic fiction usually unites detailed documentation of the more sensationalistic aspects of experience with heavily ideological (often allegorical) themes, the burden of these themes being the demonstration that man is more circumscribed than ordinarily assumed. The two large ideas which

emerged out of my examination of American novels of this kind
since the early 1890s are that these works frequently contain significant tragic themes (I discuss my notion of naturalistic tragedy
in my introduction and return to it often elsewhere), and that they
fall into three distinct groups—the three waves of major novels by
major new novelists in the 1890s, the 1930s, and the late 1940s and
early 1950s. (It was this realization which helped determine the
organization of my study.)

The reappearance of naturalism at several points in our literary
history suggests that it has survived as a significant yet popular
literary movement in America because it has responded to the
preoccupations of particular moments of modern American life
and has discovered appropriate forms for doing so. My task as an
interpreter of this phenomenon was therefore threefold. I had to
seek to identify the characteristics of naturalistic fiction at the particular moments during which the movement flourished in order
to distinguish the distinctive qualities which crested during that
decade. I had to confirm and identify more clearly than in my
working hypothesis those characteristics which appear in naturalistic fiction from decade to decade and which thus represent the
sustaining base of the movement. And I had to attempt to establish
the relation between the naturalism of specific works and the permanent fictional worth of these works.

The late nineteenth-century phase of American naturalism has
been fully studied by a number of critics,[10] including myself.[11] But
the naturalism of the 1930s and of the late 1940s and early
1950s—are many of the major works of these periods naturalistic,
and if so in what ways?—is still a largely unexplored area of in-
quiry. In particular, some of the best fiction of the late 1940s and
early 1950s has still to be adequately described as a third significant phase of naturalism in America. I have therefore divided my
study into three unequal parts. The first contains an introduction
to literary naturalism in the 1890s which concentrates on those aspects of the naturalism of the decade which are pertinent to the
movement as a whole. The other two parts contain brief prefatory
accounts of the two twentieth-century phases of American naturalism and full discussions of six novels which I believe constitute the
best fiction written in the naturalistic tradition during these
phases.

This method perhaps requires a further word of explanation.
The ideological burden of the study is contained in the introduc-

tion and later prefaces and in the illustration of the ideas of these section in the explication of specific novels. I have not sought to write a study in which—as is frequent in discussions of American naturalism—the examination of the fiction itself is subordinate to a constant reference to philosophical and cultural ideas. I have rather attempted to see if literary criticism can make a contribution to a particularly muddled area of literary history.

The novels which I have chosen to discuss at length are, for the 1930s, James T. Farrell's *Studs Lonigan*, John Dos Passos' *U.S.A.*, and John Steinbeck's *The Grapes of Wrath*; and, for the late 1940s and early 1950s, Norman Mailer's *The Naked and the Dead*, William Styron's *Lie Down in Darkness*, and Saul Bellow's *The Adventures of Augie March*. This selection is of course arbitrary but is neverthe-less defensible. The novels chosen are major works by major twen-tieth-century American naturalists—in most instances *the* major work. No doubt there is much of interest and worth in the best novels of a number of other writers who are often identified as twentieth-century American naturalists, such as Richard Wright, Erskine Caldwell, John O'Hara, Nelson Algren, and James Jones. But most of these figures are clearly of second rank, and one, Wright, is a major figure whose principal naturalistic novel, *Native Son*, is a seriously flawed work. My choice also arises out of a dis-inclination to examine yet again a number of the frequently expli-cated novels of Hemingway and Faulkner. Several strains in their fiction can be profitably studied in relation to the naturalistic movement in America, but that task belongs to a different kind of book than the one I have written. I am, in brief, offering an inter-pretation of American naturalism in the twentieth century which is derived not from a survey of the entire field but from a close study of the best and most significant novels in the movement.

Acknowledgments

I wish to thank the National Endowment for the Humanities for a fellowship which allowed me the time to prepare and write this study. As always, I have profited greatly from the editorial skill of my wife, Carol.

A version of the essay on James T. Farrell was read at the Fifth Alabama Symposium on Literature in October 1979. Portions of the Preface, Introduction, and Postscript have appeared, in much different form, in my essays "Nineteenth-Century American Naturalism: An Approach Through Form," *Forum* (Houston), 13 (Winter 1976): 43–46; "American Literary Naturalism: The Example of Dreiser," *Studies in American Fiction*, 5 (Spring 1977): 41–63; and "American Literary Naturalism and the Humanistic Tradition," The Andrew W. Mellon Lecture, Tulane University, Spring 1978. I wish to thank the editors of these journals and the Tulane University Graduate School for permission to reprint this material.

Twentieth-Century American Literary Naturalism

Introduction

American Naturalism in the 1890s

There is no need to discuss in detail the conditions and ideas which contributed to the development of a new literary sensibility in the 1890s.[1] Most students of American life are familiar with the premise that the 1890s were in fact distinguished less by major social and intellectual changes than by a full realization of changes which had occurred during the previous two decades—in particular, the rapid shift from a predominantly rural, agrarian civilization to an urban, industrial society, and the transition from traditional religious faith and moral belief to skepticism and uncertainty.

The realization by the generation coming of age in the 1890s that American life had changed radically since the Civil War helped compromise a key aspect of the American Dream—the faith that America guaranteed all men the free and just pursuit of self-fulfillment and of the good life. William Dean Howells' *The Rise of Silas Lapham*, published in 1885, is perhaps the last major endorsement of the operative truth of this faith. Howells' story of a Vermont farmer who discovers a paint mine on his property and who builds a successful business in the city without losing his moral honesty and courage affirms the unity of the ethical and material life in America. Silas, however, must eventually sacrifice his wealth and position to maintain his honesty, a sacrifice which reflects Howells' recognition of the increasing destructive strength of the new urban business civilization in which his Vermont farmer finds himself.

Howells and his generation—the generation as well of Mark Twain and Henry James, all of whom were born in the late 1830s or early 1840s—maintained in varying degrees the ethical idealism of the pre-industrial, pre-Darwinian America of their youth. A career such as Silas's reflects the hope that the average American can still "rise" to ethical courage despite the largely corrupt world in which he lives. But the generation of Stephen Crane, Frank Norris, and Theodore Dreiser (the generation of the early 1870s) found a hope of this kind not so much invalid as extraneous. City-wise (if not entirely city-bred), they believed that contemporary America was a closed rather than an open society and that life in this society was characterized by a struggle to survive materially rather than to prevail morally. Great industrial and financial combinations and self-serving national political parties appeared to control the fate of the nation as a whole, while the destiny of the common man of city and town—a destiny powerfully influenced by his personal and social background—appeared to be equally beyond individual control. The feeling was that man was limited, shaped, conditioned—determined, if you will—and the search was for appropriate symbolic constructs to express this sense. A half-understood Darwinism and a too-readily absorbed Spencerianism supplied one core of metaphor and symbol, and a crudely applied machine analogy the other. "Environment is a tremendous thing in the world and frequently shapes lives regardless,"[2] Stephen Crane wrote in 1893 in explanation of his theme in *Maggie*, a work in which he offered an animalistic slum as a controlling symbol, while in *The Red Badge of Courage* he was to speak of man trapped in the "moving box" of "iron laws of tradition and law."[3] Theodore Dreiser caught the drift of this view of man's condition in a characteristic blending of the cosmic and bathetic. "Among the forces which sweep and play throughout the universe," he wrote in *Sister Carrie*, "untutored man is but a wisp in the wind."[4]

Of course, young writers of the 1890s were aided in their understanding of "forces" by the work of Emile Zola and other late nineteenth-century European realists and naturalists. By the 1890s, Zola had wide currency in America, whether one read him avidly in the original French, as did Norris, or came to his ideas and interests indirectly, as did Crane and Dreiser.[5] Zola's revolt against romantic idealism, his acceptance of the grandiose claims of mid-nineteenth century scientism, and his dismay over the social and political corruption of Second-Empire France were responses to conditions of his day (conditions paralleled in 1890s America) which helped shape a view of literature in which man's pride in his distinctiveness had little place. Fiction, Zola believed, should above all be truthful rather than polite, amusing, or ennobling, and truth was achieved by depicting life in accord with scientific laws and methods—a goal which to Zola in the 1870s had about it the aura of a postmortem dissection of a diseased corpse.

But present as well in this attitude, and feeding its intensity, were Zola's powerful anti-clerical and anti-establishment beliefs. His scientism, in short, had at its roots a deep Enlightenment distrust of the supernatural and of the ways in which religious belief in particular often buttressed corrupt and weak social structures. Science, to Zola, was thus a form of faith, since he believed he was using its ideals and methods to achieve a more truthful account of the human condition.

The fiction of the first generation of American naturalists suggests the ways in which Zola and the naturalistic movement were absorbed and maintained in American literary expression. The work of Crane, Norris, and Dreiser in the 1890s has many of the obvious characteristics of Zolaesque naturalism. These writers also depict contemporary middle- and lower-class life free from superficial notions of the ideal and supernatural as controlling forces in experience, and they too find man limited by the violent and irrational within himself and by the oppressive restrictions within society. But aside from these overarching similarities to Zola and to each other, each writer is very much his own man. Each explores a different aspect of American life through his own imaginative response to his world rather than in accord with a pattern and philosophy established by Zola. Each responds, in other words, to the contemporary belief that the novel was the literary form especially capable of exploring neglected areas of the interaction between social reality and the inner life and that Zola was not the model for this effort but rather the leading wedge in a progressive literary movement.

The genius of American naturalism thus lies in the looseness and freedom with which American writers dealt with the gospel according to a European prophet. It was Zola's broad impulse toward depicting truthfully all ranges of life rather than his distinctive philosophy or literary method which was the source of the strength and persistence of the movement in America. American writers were moved by an excitement born of discovering meaning and form for themselves when they began, in the 1890s, to write of the twisted and meager lives of immigrant slum dwellers, of the easy slide into the illicit by young country girls in the city and by middle-aged bar managers desiring young country girls, and of the daily grind yet sporadic violent upheavals of lower-middle-class existence. Above all, these writers no longer accepted the "great lie" of nineteenth-century fiction—the convention that insofar as literary art is concerned relations between the sexes consist either of high romantic love or the minor rituals of middle-class courtship and marriage. Sex begins in their fiction to emerge as the great theme of modern art—the dynamic center of man's tragic nature as well as the subterranean living stream of his daily life.

The ideological core of American naturalism—a sense of man more circumscribed than conventionally acknowledged—does not precede this exploration of the "low" and "irrational" but rather derives from it. Naturalistic writers found that the poor—in education, intellect, and worldly goods—are indeed pushed and forced, that the powerful do control the weak, that few men can overcome the handicaps imposed upon them by inadequacies of body and mind, and that many men have instinctive needs which are not amenable to moral suasion or rational argument. But this observation of life as it is among the lowly—because it is not abstractly derived—does not produce a simple and single deterministic creed. Compassion for the fallen, hope of betterment for the lot of the oppressed, bitterness toward the remediable which lies unremedied—all the emotions which derive from a writer's sense that he is not a dispassionate observer of a scientific process but instead an imaginative presence infusing meaning and dignity and a sense of tragic potential into what he observes—create a living engagement between artist and subject matter which results in a fullness and complexity of expression rather than an emotionally sterile portrait of "forces at work."

This fullness and complexity characterize the tragic themes which are at the heart of American naturalism—both the naturalism of the 1890s and of later generations. One such theme is that of the waste of individual potential because of the conditioning forces of life. The notion that waste constitutes a tragic condition differs markedly from the Aristotelian belief that tragedy encompasses the fall of a noble man. The Aristotelian tragic hero has already reached full stature; his fall moves us because he is a man of worth who nevertheless is brought low. The naturalistic tragic hero is a figure whose potential for growth is evident but who fails to develop because of the circumstances of his life. Stephen Crane, the 1890s writer perhaps most sensitive to the fundamental beliefs of his period, begins to explore this theme in *Maggie* (in the capacity of Maggie and Jimmie to respond to beauty),[6] and it receives major statement in the two great American naturalistic tragedies of the unfulfilled common man, *An American Tragedy* and *Studs Lonigan.*

Another important tragic theme within naturalism arises out of the failure of comparatively "successful" but essentially undistinguished figures to maintain in a shifting, uncertain world the order and stability they require to survive. The tragic effect here is again not Aristotelian; such characters as McTeague, Hurstwood, and the Joads do not fall from high place. Rather, they are wrenched by their desires or by other uncontrollable circumstances from their grooved but satisfying paths into the chaos of life "outside." They fall from midway—midway both in mind and status—rather than from a height.

A third tragic naturalistic theme concerns the problem of knowledge. The Aristotelian tragic hero may fail to understand himself or his condition during his descent, but he does in the end "discover" who he is and what has caused his fall. In the 1890s the weakening of a supernaturally sanctioned faith and the decline as well of belief in other transcendentally derived truths cast doubt on the ability of man to have a clear sense of himself in a complex and constantly shifting world. The allegorical setting of *The Red Badge of Courage* provides a powerful image of this condition. Man is alone and doubtful in an unknown world of struggle, yet he still searches in himself and in experience for confirmation of a traditional value—courage in this instance. In the end, he may believe he has discovered truth but neither Crane nor we are sure. Knowledge is now elusive, shifting, and perhaps even non-existent except for solipsistic "certainties," but man's tragic fate is still to yearn for it, as Sergeant Croft and Augie March will also yearn in later years.

These important attempts in the 1890s to redefine the tragic experience help explain the paradox I noted in my preface—the apparent contradiction between critical hostility to naturalism and the permanence and hold of the movement. On the one hand, the man of letters is troubled by the failure of naturalistic tragedy (that is, a fiction depicting the fall of man) to conform to an Aristotelian notion of the nature of tragedy, and he is also affronted by the apparent demeaning of man in naturalistic fiction. On the other hand, several generations of readers of naturalistic fiction have grasped the validity and centrality of the naturalistic effort to adapt the theme of man's sense of his own importance yet of his

propensity to fall (the essence of the tragic vision of life) to the
conditions of modern American life. The American naturalistic
tragic hero is not a noble figure who falls from high place and then
discovers the reason for his fall. Because we are a society still committed to the dream of full development of each man's potential
for the good life, we find it more moving to dramatize the crushing
or blocking of the potential for fineness of mind and spirit than
the loss of qualities already achieved. Because we are a nation
which has celebrated fraternity as a democratic ideal, we are
moved more by the destruction of one of our fellows than by the
fall of the great of our society. And because we have believed that
certain truths are universal, permanent, and comprehensible, we
are moved by the realization that we can seldom know anything
other than our own desires. No wonder that naturalism "refuses
to die."

The form of the naturalistic novel in the 1890s as well as in later
generations also reveals the capacity of naturalism to adapt a European source—in this instance the Zolaesque formula of massive
documentation and a sensationalistic plot—to the specific needs of
American life. In the America of the 1890s the need was above all
for a device which would permit the full recording of new ranges
of American experience and reveal as well the underlying nature
of this experience. The need, in short, was for the symbolic and
allegorical to reemerge as major forms of expression. Not that
these are lacking in Zola; both the repetitive concrete detail and
the sensationalism of Zola's novels contribute to a tendency toward
symbolic expression in his fiction.[7] In American naturalism this
tendency flowered into a powerful and all-pervasive tool which
frequently pushes the American naturalistic novel into allegory.
From *The Octopus* to *U.S.A.* and from *The Grapes of Wrath* to *The
Naked and the Dead* and *The Adventures of Augie March*, American
naturalists have sought to depict American life with a grandiosity
of sweep and a largeness of meaning which has made the modern
American naturalistic novel our epic literature.

Since the underlying theme of much American naturalistic fiction is the tragic incompleteness of life—how little we are or know,
despite our capacity to be and our desire to know—it is not surprising that the shape of the allegorical representation of man's
fate in the naturalistic novel of the 1890s is often of the circular
journey, of the return to our starting point, with little gained or
understood despite our movement through space and time. The

effect of this symbolic structure is to suggest that not only are human beings flawed and unfulfilled but that experience itself does not guide, instruct, or judge human nature. One of the principal corollaries of a progressive view of time is the belief that man has the ability to interact meaningfully with his world and to benefit from this interaction. But the effect of the naturalistic novel is to reverse or heavily qualify this expectation. McTeague, Sister Carrie, and Henry Fleming are, in a sense, motionless in time. They have moved through experience but still only dimly comprehend it and themselves, and thus their journeys through time are essentially circular journeys which return them to where they began. McTeague returns to the mountains of his youth and responds brutishly to their primeval enmity; Carrie still rocks and dreams of a happiness she is never to gain; and Fleming is again poised between gratuitous self-assurance and half-concealed doubt.

The form of the naturalistic novel of the 1890s thus engages us in a somewhat different aesthetic experience than does the form of a typical eighteenth- or nineteenth-century novel. Whatever the great range of theme and effect of earlier novels, we are more or less elevated by our experience of their imagined worlds. That deeply gratifying sense of knowing so well the characters of a novel that we are unwilling to part from them at the close of the book is one of the principal effects of a fiction in which the confident moral vision of the writers has encouraged him to depict life with richness and direction—with a sense, in short, that experience has a kind of describable weight and value. But the form of the naturalistic novel begins to create an effect of uncertainty, of doubt and perplexity, about whether anything can be gained or learned from experience—indeed, of doubt whether experience has any meaning aside from the existential value of a collision with phenomena.

If the form of the naturalistic novel of the 1890s is to be properly understood, however, it is necessary to qualify a view which maintains that its major impact is that of the inefficacy of time. For while the naturalistic novel does reflect a vast skepticism about the conventional attributes of experience, it also affirms the significance and worth of the seeking temperament, of the character who continues to look for meaning in experience even though there probably is no meaning. This quality appears most clearly in Dreiser's portrayal of Carrie, as it does later in Bellow's characterization of Augie. Carrie, whatever the triviality of her earlier quest or the fatuousness of her final vision, still continues to seek the meaning she calls happiness. It is present in a more tenuous form in the fact that Henry has survived his first battle—that is, his first encounter with life in all its awesome complexity—and is undismayed by the experience. And it exists faintly in the recollection we bring to McTeague's fate of his earlier responsiveness to the promise of Trina's sensuality and to the minor pleasures of middle-class domesticity. So the Carrie who rocks, the Fleming who is proud of his red badge, and the McTeague who stands clutching his gold in the empty desert represent both the inability of experience to supply a meaningful answer to the question which is human need and the tragic worth of the seeking, feeling mind.

Naturalism as it emerges in the 1890s thus takes on a configuration central to the movement as a whole in America. The naturalistic novelist is willing to concede that there are fundamental limitations to man's freedom but he is unwilling to concede that man is thereby stripped of all value. In particular, he finds significant the human drive to understand if not to control and he finds tragic the human capacity, whatever one's class or station, to suffer pain and defeat. In the 1890s the expression of these themes in naturalistic fiction is often fuzzy, as is frequently true of the early stages of any new literary movement, when strength of rebellion rather than clarity of affirmation is the principal goal. During the next two major phases of the movement in America—the 1930s and the late 1940s and early 1950s—the naturalistic novel assumes in each decade both a more clearly focused depiction of the tragic nature of experience and a depiction closely attuned to the distinctive concerns of that decade.

The 1930S

Preface

Naturalistic fiction of the 1930s has its roots in the social conditions of the decade and in the intellectual and literary currents of the previous decade.[1] James T. Farrell, John Dos Passos, and John Steinbeck did not look to the naturalists of the 1890s for their inspiration but rather found it in 1920s ideas about life and literature, ideas which helped them to explain and to express the seemingly imminent collapse of the American system in the 1930s. As early as the boom of the late 1920s many writers were beginning to feel that the average American was excessively shaped in belief and action by American economic values and practices even when he profited from this control. The depression clarified and intensified this conviction. (It is useful to recall that two of the most powerful indictments of American middle class life and its capitalistic foundation, *U.S.A.* and *Studs Lonigan*, were begun in the late twenties, before the crash.) The reappearance of naturalistic themes in the fiction of the 1930s is conventionally attributed to the heavy freight of Marxist and Freudian ideas which writers of the age carried. Marxism, like Spencerianism in the 1890s, revealed the insignificance of the individual in the process (then evolutionary, now economic) of which he was a part; Freudianism, like atavism in the 1890s, stressed the presence in man's unconscious of a controlling past. But in fact the basic beliefs of Farrell, Dos Passos, and Steinbeck were affected less by these abstract deterministic ideas than by their oblique expression in such fiction of the 1920s as James Joyce's *Ulysses*, Sherwood Anderson's *Winesburg, Ohio*, and Theodore Dreiser's *An American Tragedy*. It was in these works that the thirties novelist found a moving representation of the theme inherent in Marxism and Freudianism that life placed tragic limitations on individual freedom, growth, and happiness. Many of the novelists of the twenties appeared to be saying that we live in a trivial, banal, and tawdry world which nevertheless encloses us and shapes our destinies. We seek to escape from this world into the inner life because only there do we seem to find the richness of feeling denied us in experience. But in fact we do not really escape. The retreat into the inner life transforms us into grotesque exaggerations of what we wish to be, or causes us (with fatal consequences) to seek the translation of fantasy into reality, or engages us in an endless search for the understanding and love denied us in life.

Some of these moving accounts of anomie in the modern world had a direct influence on the naturalists of the 1930s. More often, however, the great fiction of the 1920s transmitted indirectly but powerfully to the next generation of writers its pervasive theme of the beleaguered but feeling consciousness in an inhospitable world. It was the fate of the writers of the 1930s to come to this theme when it seemed to be not merely one of the truths of experience but the only truth. The crisis in American social life in the 1930s thus joined with the naturalistic tendencies in much of the fiction of the previous decade to help form a new flowering of the naturalistic novel.

"New flowering" implies not only repetition but a degree of innovation. One important area of innovation was the form of the naturalistic novel in the 1930s. The age was affected by a desire to believe in the unity of the national experience because of the commonality of the national disaster. We are made one by our tragic condition and we must therefore find ways to dramatize this awful unity. Writers struggled to create forms which would express this sense of oneness. Dos Passos sought to emulate in *U.S.A.* the formal conventions of the epic in range and in the representation of a national ethos. Farrell in *Studs Lonigan* worked in detail with a narrow segment of life with a conscious effort to achieve the effect of a microcosm in which the minutely observed would suggest the whole of which it was a reflection. And Steinbeck in *The Grapes of Wrath* combined these two devices. The Biblical exodus overstructure of the Joads' journey implied a universality to their plight, while the interlacing of detailed accounts of their movements with the impersonal "interchapters" established a macrocosm-microcosm effect.

This desire to render through form a belief in the universality of the American dilemma is closely related to the heavy ideological burden of the 1930s naturalistic novel. The writer wished to communicate something important about all of American life, and this intent pushed him toward allegory as a means of achieving thematic clarity and strength. Yet he also wished to probe inwardly, to tell us about the individual consciousness within the "system" as a

ost of the manuscripts were written with the ideal of ob-
ctivity in mind. I realized then that the writer should sub-
it himself to an objective discipline.[3]

onigan appears to confirm the belief that one of Farrell's
bjects in his early work was to document the sensationally
ing in life. In the area of sexual experience alone, for ex-
Studs Lonigan presents us with whores and whorehouses,
bation, homosexuality and lesbianism, rape, adultery, inces-
onging, venereal disease, and unwanted pregnancy.
ell has been aware of the superficial and reductive reputa-
f Studs Lonigan as a "dirty book" about the Chicago slums
g the depression. He has sought to explain that Studs, though
a first generation Chicago Irish neighborhood, deals largely
ower middle class families (Studs' father is a painting con-
r and a landlord), that only Judgment Day occurs during the
ssion, and that the sexual and other seemingly extraordinary
rial in the trilogy is typical of the characters and their world.[4]
e all, Farrell has attempted to explain that Studs Lonigan is a
l which is devoted not to a documentation of externals but
r to a representation of the inner life. He wrote in his 1938
duction to the Modern Library edition of the trilogy that
ls was "a normal American boy" who was bred in a milieu of
ritual poverty" and that in the course of his life "his values
ome the values of his world."[5] And he noted in 1948 that his
rt in the work was to write "mainly from the standpoint of im-
diate experiences. By that I mean this: any event which appears
he book is presented in terms of . . . how it registers upon the
sciousness of one or more of the characters."[6]
These accounts by Farrell of his intent in Studs Lonigan locate
center of the trilogy in the 1920s belief that it is the novelist's
nction to commit himself to the dramatization of the inner life
hat Farrell calls the "spiritual") as that life interacts with a social
ality which informs and often collides with it. Of course, most
tion in one way or another is devoted to the depiction of the
lationship between distinctive temperaments and a particular-
ed outer world. But the fictional form given this relationship
hanges from age to age, and in the 1920s the forms which were
oth most characteristic among major writers and most influential
n Farrell were those of James Joyce and Sherwood Anderson.
Farrell himself has noted the powerful effect these writers had

way of informing us about the system. This, too, had been Crane's
intent in The Red Badge of Courage, a novel in which Henry's consciousness is the focus within an allegorically shaded action. But
whereas Crane's allegory is fuzzy and ambivalent and his depiction
of Henry's mind often fumbling, the typical naturalistic novelist of
the 1930s presents both a more tightly structured and more apparent allegory and a more sophisticated rendering of psychological
reality. Dos Passos' Camera Eye and Farrell's indirect discourse
technique draw upon some thirty years of experimentation by
twentieth-century novelists with devices for the dramatization of
the inner life.

The emphasis of naturalistic tragedy in the 1930s on the waste
of the individual capacity for the good life emerges out of the
naturalist's depiction of the interaction between an operative social
morality and the thwarted self. Crudely stated, Studs, the Joads,
and Charley Anderson fail because they live in a society in which
mass values—principally those of a competitive and exploitative
capitalism but also of other kinds—shape their lives. The theme of
the destruction of the individual by a group value contains, however, the counter-theme of the potential for growth by those who
realize that there is a beneficial strength in a mass ethos when it is
used to protect and nurture rather than control the individual.
This interplay between a destructive possessiveness and a beneficial sharing is central to The Grapes of Wrath, in which the Joads
move from the mass ethic of familial and personal self-centered-
ness (the "I") to an acceptance of responsibility for the well-being
of all men (the "We"). It is also a major element in several strands
of U.S.A. (a number of the biographies and all of the Camera Eye)
which attempt to revivify the dream of an ideal democracy in
which each man's freedom depends on his willingness to defend
the freedom of all. And it is present in Studs Lonigan in that Studs'
self-destructive narrowness derives from his failure to experience
a wider world.

The insight that in the group or society as a whole there is not
only confinement but the possible release from confinement is ac-
quired by a character of sensibility and feeling in the course of the
novel. In the naturalistic novel of the 1930s, unlike that of the
1890s, knowledge is difficult but achievable. The greater difficulty
now is doing. Characters such as the Camera Eye persona, Tom
and Ma Joad, and even Studs come at last to know themselves and
their worlds, but knowledge is not power but rather the tragic ac-

companiment of weakness. Nevertheless, the basic cast of the naturalistic novel of the 1930s—the diagnosis of an illness and the suggestion of a remedy—creates an effect different from that of the naturalistic novel of the 1890s. The concluding impression is not now one of circularity, of blankness and puzzlement as McTeague returns to the mountains or Fleming reckons up his growth. It is rather an effect of understanding and therefore of an element of hope as the Camera Eye realizes we are two nations, as Tom undertakes his discipleship of activism, and as Danny O'Neill emerges with a clear vision out of the same world which produced Studs. A permanent naturalistic theme—the capacity of men of all stations to feel deeply—is now expanded into an ability to understand as well, and in understanding there is promise for the future.

In its theme of hope from out of the ruins, the naturalistic novel of the 1930s evokes one of the principal attitudes of the decade, just as naturalistic fiction of the 1890s reflects the confusion and ambivalence of that moment. For as Richard Pells, among others, has noted, the chaos and turmoil of the social collapse of the 1930s did not cause despair among writers and intellectuals but rather the vitalizing expectation that out of the rubble of the old system and its values would emerge a society more capable of fulfilling the American dream.[2] As Farrell succinctly put it, he wrote *Studs Lonigan* as "an oblique expression of the fact that I have faith in man and I have faith in the future."[3]

Studs Loni

Studs Lonigan was begun in June 1929,
first two novels—*Young Lonigan* and *The*
Lonigan—were largely completed by mid
hood of Studs Lonigan ends on New Year's D
ume of the trilogy, *Judgment Day*, is set dur
against a background of a collapsed mar
businesses, strikes, mass unemployment,
agitation that Studs moves toward his death
more documentary in technique than the
drawing heavily on the use of headlines, son
manner of Dos Passos. The powerful impa
subject matter and documentary method, as
matic dreariness and failure of Studs' life, has
of *Studs Lonigan* as the archetypal thirties nov
principal intent is to portray in detail the tr
American society during the decade.[2]

Another common impression of Farrell's tri
pose is to dramatize the sordid and degrading
ence. Farrell's early work often does tend in th
himself noted in an account of his experiments
up to *Studs Lonigan*. Many of these pieces, he rec

related to death, disintegration, human i
drunkenness, ignorance, human cruelty. T
describe dusty and deserted streets, stre
erable homes, pool rooms, brothels, dance h
bohemian sections, express offices, gasoline
scenes laid in slum districts. The characters
gangs, drunkards, Negroes, expressmen, ho
migrants and immigrant landlords, filling-s
ants, straw bosses, hitch hikers, bums, bewil

upon him during the period he was forming his literary sensibility and fictional method in the late 1920s. As an author concerned with the inhospitality of Irish-American lower middle class culture to the life of the mind and spirit, Farrell could not help being drawn to similar themes in Joyce. More significantly, he was especially attracted—as were so many others of his generation—by Joyce's striking portrayal of the interplay between the minutiae of everyday life and the individual consciousness. It was this aspect of Joyce which Farrell stressed in his *A Note on Literary Criticism* of 1936 when he sought to defend Joyce's work against its simple-minded dismissal by Marxist critics and to place it affirmatively within the development of naturalism. Naturalism, Farrell noted, had begun as a fiction of "extensiveness"—that is, as a fiction devoted to the depiction of a panoramic social milieu. In the work of Joyce it had progressed to a fiction of "intensity," in which the novelist represented both a narrower and more minutely caught social world and "the individual consciousness."[7] Indeed, if Farrell had wished, he could have offered as additional evidence of this progress his own work of Joycean naturalism, the novel *Gas-House McGinty*.

Gas-House McGinty was written in mid-1931, in Paris, after Farrell had completed drafts of the first two volumes of *Studs Lonigan* but before he had begun *Judgment Day*. *Gas-House McGinty* is in part a 1930s slice-of-life novel. Set principally in the dispatcher's office of a large express company, it renders in mind-numbing repetitive detail the noise, horse-play, bickering, small-mindedness, and prejudices of men at work. McGinty is a leading figure in the office, and our impression of him in this context is of grossness and inflated self-importance. But McGinty also has an active though usually repressed aesthetic sensibility and a great need to be loved, qualities of his inner life which express themselves in his enthusiasm for the elegance and beauty of applied mathematics—what McGinty calls "figures worked out"[8]—and in the wild fantasizing of his dream life.

Farrell later noted that the impulse behind the long chapter in *Gas-House McGinty* in which he presented a surrealistic account of one of McGinty's dreams was his desire to experiment with this form of material before exploiting it at even greater length and complexity in the portion of *Judgment Day* he intended to devote to Studs' death-bed delirium.[9] The Joycean model for fiction of this kind—the nighttown episode in *Ulysses*—is clear enough. What is perhaps less clear is that in both *Gas-House McGinty* and *Studs Lonigan* Farrell's desire to work closely with the paradoxes offered by a mundane and restrictive outer world and an emotionally vital inner life was also influenced by the work of Sherwood Anderson.

Farrell has often commented on his debt to Anderson, perhaps most explicitly in 1954, when he noted that Anderson "influenced and inspired me perhaps more profoundly than any other American writer." It was not only Anderson's sympathy in *Winesburg* for "the grotesque, the queer, the socially abnormal" which moved Farrell, but more significantly—as Farrell realized in 1927 after reading Anderson's autobiography *Tar*—his concern for "the inner life of a boy in an Ohio country town." Farrell intuitively felt, he recalled, that in Anderson's work he was discovering the potential source of his own art. "Perhaps my own feelings and emotions," he wrote, "and the feelings and emotions of those with whom I had grown up were important. . . . I thought of writing a novel about my own boyhood, about the neighborhood in which I had grown up. Here was one of the seeds that led to *Studs Lonigan*." [10]

Joyce and Anderson had a number of distinctive meanings for Farrell. Joyce confirmed Farrell's awareness of the potential for satire and burlesque in the pompous self-certainties of middle-class Irish life. And Anderson helped shape Farrell's understanding of the deformities of character which occur when the human need for love is frustrated. But together the two represent as well a powerful single impulse toward the depiction of the inner life as this quality exists in conjunction with a social world which provides little for the cultivation and satisfaction of man's "spiritual" nature.

The extraordinary fullness of naturalistic detail in *Studs Lonigan* can therefore best be understood not as an end in itself—to document a specific world—but rather as a device to clothe and express what in essence is a tragic morality play. By this I mean that the substance of *Studs Lonigan*—its characters, setting, and events—is structured as a moral allegory in which all that the Everyman protagonist encounters in experience is directly related to his potential damnation or salvation. In *Studs Lonigan*, however, "damnation" is not a conventional religious belief but rather the naturalistic theme of the tragic waste of a potentially fruitful life and sensibility.

As Farrell has explained many times, he is not a determinist. He rather accepted the pragmatic social philosophy of John Dewey and George Herbert Mead which he encountered at the University of Chicago in the late 1920s. He thus believed that a truthful fictional portrayal of life is not a matter of plotting the effect of social and natural forces upon an individual but of recognizing in his development the constant and fluid interaction between specific qualities of temperament and experience.[11] Farrell's conception and dramatization of life are thus dualistic. The individual encounters in his experience that which either contributes to his growth, given his own distinctive character and circumstances, or inhibits it. Because of the humanistic cast of both pragmatic philosophy and Farrell's fundamental frame of mind, this dualism has a moral character. That which aids in the growth of mind and spirit is "good," that which restricts or imprisons or retards is "evil." It is this aspect of Farrell's ideas which results in the morality play quality of *Studs Lonigan*. Almost every detail in the trilogy exists in relation to the allegorical theme of the spiritual health of a particular soul in its journey through life.

We first encounter Studs at fourteen smoking a forbidden cigarette in the bathroom of his home on the eve of his graduation from grammar school. While practicing twisting his "frank and boyish face" into "tough-guy sneers,"[12] he indulges in a long reverie about his years at St. Patrick's parochial school. Studs' free-flowing recollections are dominated, as they will be through most of his life, by the figures of Lucy Scanlan and Weary Reilley. Lucy causes in him "all kinds of goofy, dizzy feelings that he liked," "flowing feelings" (YL, 7, 8) that move him deeply even though he cannot begin to understand them. His reponse to her, as we come to understand more fully during the following summer, is not merely an adolescent sexual awakening but also a dawning of his capacity for affection and love and for a corresponding grasping of the spirit of beauty in life. Studs' thoughts about Weary, in contrast, are single-minded and clear. Weary is "one tough customer" (YL, 6) whom Studs hates because Weary is his principal rival in the struggle for prominence within the adolescent masculine competitive world of the school.

Lucy and Weary are polar opposites in relation to Studs. Lucy, because she offers to Studs an opportunity for expression of his deepest nature through communion with others, constitutes his potential for growth. Weary, because he represents Studs' conformity to a mindless street ethic of hardness, cruelty, and power, constitutes his potential for permanent adolescence and eventual self-destruction. The two figures, both in their appearances in Studs' life and in their roles as reference points of emotion and value in his reveries, thus function like the "good" and "evil" angels in a medieval morality play. Lucy is spirit, Weary the world; Lucy speaks to Studs' inner ear of love, Weary of pride.

Young Lonigan is devoted to the depiction of Studs' life during the summer after his graduation and in particular to the two major events which represent the temporary balance between the major poles of attraction in his life. The first event is a fight with Weary, observed by Studs' street world, in which Studs is victorious. Studs feels that his conquest of Weary is a turning point in his life. "He was going to be an important guy, and all the punks would look up to him . . . and he would be . . . in the limelight. Maybe it would set things happening as he always knew they would; and he would keep on getting more and more important" (YL, 87). Shortly afterwards Studs and Lucy spend a long idyllic afternoon in Washington Park, sitting in a tree and talking. The moment moves Studs to a series of poetic visions: that the "wind was Lucy's hand caressing his hair" and that "the sounds of the park . . . seemed as if they were all, somehow, part of himself, and he was part of them, and them and himself were free from the drag of his body that had aches and dirty thoughts, and got sick, and could only be in one place at a time" (YL, 111, 112). They kiss, and Studs feels that this, too, is a turning point, that "from now on everything was going to be jake" (YL, 112). And when they part that evening, "She stood a moment on the porch, smiling at him through the summer dusk; and the spray from the sprinkler on her lawn tapped her cheeks; the boy, Studs, saw and felt something beautiful and vague, something like a prayer sprung into flesh" (YL, 115).

The two "turning points" are at once irreconcilable and unevenly matched, since Studs' sharply defined and powerful street ethic cannot accept his inadequately realized and "soft" spiritual needs and desires. At the first sign of opposition between the two poles of value—a number of childishly scribbled "Studs loves Lucy" graffiti—Studs rejects his relationship with Lucy as unbecoming his public role. Farrell at this point spells out openly the allegorical nature of the contest: "The old feeling for Lucy flowed through him, warm. She seemed to him like a . . . like a saint or a beautiful queen, or a goddess. But the tough outside part of Studs told the tender inside part of him that nobody really knew, that he had better forget all that bull. He tried to, and it wasn't very easy" (YL, 139).

Almost every other aspect of the trilogy—not merely of *Young Lonigan*—can be related to the opposing clusters of value represented by Lucy and Weary. Helen Shires is a figure parallel to Lucy. She is a tomboy who offers Studs understanding and comradeship (though not on the mystical level of his response to Lucy) unavailable in his more guarded and competitive relationships with his street gang. Lucy and Helen live on Indiana Street; most of Studs' gang, including Weary, live near Fifty-eight Street and Prairie and use that corner and the poolroom and coffee shop on Prairie as gathering places. Studs' neighborhood is close to Washington Park and not far from Lake Michigan, and these too take on symbolic meanings. The park has a dual capacity. In the park, the gang members, including Studs, can display their various street roles, but Studs alone can reach out for larger meanings. Even late in his life, when wandering in Washington Park, Studs can experience again the kind of mystical insight he had had there with Lucy: "He was humble and soft, and felt there was something behind all this that he saw, sun, and sky, and new grass, and trees . . . and it was God. God made all this, moved it, made it live. . . . And God was the spirit behind it all and behind everything" (JD, 189).

Characters, activities, and setting are thus all part of the iconographic texture of *Studs Lonigan*. Around Fifty-eighth and Prairie cluster Weary, Red Kelly, Tommy Doyle, Shrimp Haggerty, and the many others of the "gang." This is a world dominated by the poolroom, by an ethic of toughness, and by activities which demonstrate hardness and manliness—earlier by street fighting and hooliganism and later by gambling, drinking, and whoring. Indiana, the park, and the lake constitute the world of Studs alone or with a companion with whom he can share his thoughts, a world in which he is capable of searching out with some honesty, though also confusedly and crudely, his feelings and needs. Often this search occurs in a natural setting or while Studs is engaged in a "natural" activity, like swimming. Indeed, Farrell is remarkably successful in finding in the heavily populated and overbuilt urban world of *Studs Lonigan* symbolic equivalents of the traditional opposition between man confined in thought and feeling by a restrictive society and man alone and free in nature.

One of Farrell's principal themes in *Studs Lonigan* is that the social institutions which should play a role in encouraging Studs to grow beyond his childish street roles and to accept the promptings of his "soft" inner nature fail to do so. Because these institutions are either irrelevant to Studs' basic dilemma or indeed confirm a tough guy ethic, Farrell's depiction of them is in the mode of Joycean surrealistic parody. He wished to capture the vacuousness, hypocrisy, and at times open malignancy of these supposedly meliorating social structures and his tone is therefore properly bitter. Studs' involvement in Home and Church is dramatized in a series of sharply satiric portraits of the platitudinous emptiness of the knowledge of self and the world which parents and clergy seek to convey to Studs. Studs' parents are preoccupied with superficial niceties of manners and morals and with totally anomalous roles for Studs (his mother wishes him to become a priest) which drive him out of the house. And the several lengthy religious scenes—Father Shannon's sermon, the Young People's Social Club, and the Order of Christopher initiation—reveal a similar preoccupation with a superficial prohibitory moralism. State and Art endorse values which validate Studs' street ethic of a mindless and destructive manliness. Thoughts of Country to Studs are linked to a feverish unthinking patriotism which expresses itself in games of war and in hate. During the Chicago Armistice Day celebration of 1918, the gang viciously beats up a drunk while Studs shouts, "That's the Fifty-eighth Street spirit" (YM, 39). And Art to Studs is the fantasy world created by popular romantic or gangster movies, a world in which he finds confirmed his belief that toughness is sexually attractive and heroic.

The pull and hold of *Studs Lonigan* as a narrative lie in the tensions which exist among the opposing clusters of value represented by Lucy and Weary. From the point early in *Young Lonigan* when Studs and Lucy spend their long afternoon in Washington Park, we want Studs to "succeed" by accepting that side of him represented by his response to Lucy and by rejecting his street code and roles. But though we want Studs to be gentle and warm and to think large thoughts about himself and experience, the direction of his life—because of the power of his street ethic and of his failure to find confirmation in his culture of his "goofy" side—is toward pursuit of "Weary" and rejection of "Lucy." The trilogy therefore contains a pervasive dramatic irony which is one of the principal sources of our involvement in Studs' life. We see clearly the potential for "good" in him which he himself fails to understand, and we thus accompany him through the largest portion of his life with the painful recognition that his failure in self-knowledge is contributing to his self-destruction.

Although Lucy and Weary remain avatars of value in Studs' consciousness throughout *Studs Lonigan*, their meaning for Studs is duplicated by other figures, activities, and settings as the trilogy progresses. In *The Young Manhood of Studs Lonigan* the mysterious blonde girl whom Studs sees in church keeps weakly alive in his imagination the possibility of gaining a Lucy-like companion. In *Judgment Day*, although Studs gains a sweetheart, he views her as an inadequate substitute for Lucy. He finds both the blonde and Catherine unsatisfactory surrogates for Lucy because they are in fact not the "real" Lucy. That is, his involvement with them does not constitute a full acceptance of himself, as his involvement with Lucy had done, but only his nostalgia for that involvement. If the possibilities of life represented by Lucy offer little satisfaction in their surrogates, the possibilities represented by Weary offer even less in their actuality. Here the morality play character of the trilogy takes on the configuration of a Rake's Progress. By midway in *The Young Manhood of Studs Lonigan*, Studs appears to have achieved all that he desired as a young adolescent. Horsing around aimlessly at street corners has been replaced by the deeply anticipated pleasures of "hanging around the poolroom, now and then a small-time crap game or round of poker; benders on Saturday night, and maybe a couple of times during the week; sometimes a can house" (YM, 146). But in fact there is no enjoyment for Studs in these activities, only slow decay and dissolution. Sex, because it is mechanical, disappoints him, and drinking makes him ill. He becomes fat and pasty, and venereal disease and bad liquor begin to break down his health. In scenes of Studs drunk and sick in bars and whorehouses, or of the gang mechanically seeking mechanical pleasures out of boredom, the trilogy becomes a parable which achieves its intent by representing the morally repellent as physically repellent.

Farrell's acount of Studs' decline also takes on shape from the changing proportion of thoughts of Lucy and of death in Studs' imagination. As Lucy fades as an achievable core of value—both in herself and in her surrogates—Studs finds himself increasingly preoccupied with thoughts of death. This preoccupation is in one sense "natural"; several of the gang suffer early death, and Studs' own health is increasingly poor. But we are also once again in the

world of moral allegory, in which Lucy is both irrecoverable past
and "life," and in which the inevitable and obsessively present consequence to the suppression of the spirit is death.

The true climax to the morality play aspect of *Studs Lonigan*,
however, is not Studs' death at the conclusion of *Judgment Day* but
the New Year's Eve party which ends *The Young Manhood of Studs
Lonigan*. By late 1928 most of the members of the gang have
moved from the Fifty-eighth and Prairie neighborhood and seldom see each other. Nevertheless, they decide to have a New Year's
Eve party in a hotel in the old neighborhood. Even before the
party begins Studs becomes drunk and mourns maudlinly for
Lucy. The party itself displays the gang in all its mindless brutality.
Men fight and are sick and girls are attacked and raped in an
epitome of Studs' street world. But the party not only symbolizes
the nature of the life which Studs has chosen to lead but the consequences of that choice. At the party the still drunken Studs is
badly beaten by Weary and wakes up the following morning, after
a night of lying unconscious outdoors, at the corner of Fifty-eighth
and Prairie seriously ill with the pneumonia which will eventually
contribute to his death. The moral allegory which is Studs' life has
now reached its proper conclusion. Lucy is lost and the goal represented by Weary gained, but this goal, in the person of Weary
himself, has also demonstrated its "evil" power over Studs' fate. So
Studs is left an empty hulk in body and soul at the scene where he
began his descent some fifteen years earlier. And so Farrell, who
usually permits the allegory to speak for itself, cannot forebear in
this climactic instance from commenting on Studs as he lies unconscious in the street. "It was Studs Lonigan, who had once, as a boy,
stood before Charley Bathcellar's poolroom thinking that some
day, he would grow up to be strong, and tough, and the real stuff"
(YM, 411).

The note of condescension and even of contempt in this authorial aside appears to be confirmed by the judgment of various
"norms" in the trilogy—by characters who seem to be speaking for
Farrell in their comments on Studs and his world. Christy, for example, is a radical intellectual Greek counterman in the coffee
shop which Studs and the gang frequent in *The Young Manhood of
Studs Lonigan*. His view of the gang is that they are "silly boys. They
have no education. They go to school to the sisters. . . . Sisters,
sanctimonious hypocrites. . . . What can they teach boys. . . . Silly
boys, they grow up, their fathers want to make money, their moth-

ers are silly women and pray like the sanctimonious sisters, hypocrites. The boys run the streets, and grow up in pool-rooms, drink and become hooligans. They don't know any better. Silly boys, and they kill themselves with diseases from whores and this gin they drink" (YM, 336). This contemptuous and unsympathetic but superficially accurate account of Studs' life is similar to the cold and bitter anger toward Studs' world expressed by another spokesman figure, Danny O'Neill. Danny has studied and has gone to college and has thus escaped the narrow vision and life of Studs. But because he has only recently escaped and because he dreams of a better world which is to replace the one from which he has escaped, he is bitter and angry. "He hated it all. It was all part of a dead world; it was filthy; it was rotten; it was stupefying" (YM, 370).

Studs Lonigan, however, is not merely a novel in which an allegory of moral retribution clothed in naturalistic detail expresses its author's contempt for his subject. If it were only this, it would not be the permanent and moving work which it has proven to be. It is also a work in which Farrell, influenced by Joyce and Anderson, seeks to make real and sympathetic the inner life of Studs and thus to enforce upon us through our understanding of him not only the justice of his fall but its tragic pathos as well. This effect is achieved in two ways—by Farrell's use of the technique of indirect discourse to render Studs' inner life, his stream of consciousness, and by his casting of the third novel in the trilogy in the form of a tragedy in which the pain and anguish suffered by the tragic protagonist in his just fall are accompanied by his growth in understanding and feeling.

It is now conventional wisdom that stream-of-consciousness fiction is not a technique but rather a subject matter which can be presented through various techniques, and that this subject matter appeared in fiction long before its vogue in experimental fiction of the 1920s.[13] We also now know, because of the recent suggestive study by Roy Pascal called *The Dual Voice*, that one of the important early modes for depicting internal states of mind and feeling is the device which Pascal names "free indirect speech"[14] and which I shall call "indirect discourse." In brief, the device of indirect discourse is that of depicting in a third person narrative voice the thoughts and feelings of a character, yet doing so, as Pascal notes, with "the vivacity of direct speech, evoking the personal tone, the gesture, and often the idiom of the . . . thinker reported."[15] The "dual voice" of the device derives from the circumstance that the narrator is present as reporter, structurer, and summarizer of the character's frame of mind but that he presents this material in the language and grammatical form habitually used by the character.

Obviously, indirect discourse is a device capable of much variation, and Pascal notes the range in its use from its occasional appearances in eighteenth-century fiction to its centrality and increasing sophistication in the nineteenth-century novel. In particular, he notes the importance of the technique in the fiction of Flaubert and Zola. Flaubert made it the means by which he depicted the inner life of his characters with a seeming authorial detachment, and Zola exploited it to lend a texture of working-class raciness and crudity to the narrative language of specific novels. In the twentieth century, in the work of Virginia Woolf, for example, the device intensifies both in the depth of psychic experience depicted and in the exclusiveness of its presence as a narrative technique.

A few examples from *Studs Lonigan* would be helpful at this point, both to suggest the nature of indirect discourse in general and to illustrate some of the distinctive uses which Farrell makes of the device. Here, for example, is Studs' father early in the trilogy ruminating on the future of his family:

> When he'd bought this building, Wabash Avenue had been a nice, decent, respectable street for a self-respecting man to live with his family. But now, well, the niggers and kikes were getting in, and they were dirty, and you didn't know but what, even in broad daylight, some nigger moron might be attacking his girls. (YL, 19)

It is clear in this passage that it is the narrator who is reporting Lonigan's thoughts, but the thoughts themselves appear in the verbal and syntactical form Lonigan himself might use if he were articulating them.

And here, in a somewhat more complex and rich example, is Studs, late in the trilogy, walking with his girl Catherine on a Sunday morning:

> Jesus, if only he could walk along with her on a sunny spring morning like this one and not have a worry in his

head, no worry about his dough sunk in Imbray stock, about his health and weak heart, and the possibility of not living a long life, and not be wondering would he, by afternoon, feel pooped and shot. And then it was so gloomy at home that it could be cut with a knife, and it was bound to affect him, the old man's business going to pot, his dough lost and going fast, his expenses, unrented apartments, the mortgage. Just to have none of these things on his mind, and to be able to stroll along Easy Street with Catherine at his side, perfectly happy all day, and not having to feel that when he woke up tomorrow all these thoughts would pop back and keep going off like fire-crackers in his mind all day. And he had to decide about holding or selling his stock. Which? (JD, 160)

The language and grammar of this passage are, as before, principally those of the mind being depicted. But the passage also now contains a free-association movement shaped and controlled by Studs' emotion of the moment—his anxiety. There is as well more rhetorical emphasis through structural parallelism and colloquial imagery ("cut with a knife," "Easy Street," "going off like fire-crackers") than would be characteristic of Studs' speech. In short, the passage seeks not only to report the details of Studs' state of mind but also, by means of authorial shaping, the emotional reality of that state. It is not Studs' mind which is speaking directly to us but rather his mind filtered through the controlling rhetorical skill of the narrator.

One might ask, if indirect discourse of this kind is the principal narrative device of *Studs Lonigan*—as indeed it is—why Farrell's participation in modern stream-of-consciousness fiction hasn't been more widely noted and discussed, particularly when Farrell himself has often commented on his efforts at a "free association" depiction of Studs' internal state and indeed once even used the term "stream of consciousness" to describe his method in the novel.[16] One reason, of course, is that Farrell's indirect discourse presents few problems in immediate apprehension and is therefore less noticeable than the free-association devices of Joyce or Faulkner or even Virginia Woolf. Another reason—and one more pertinent for our purposes—is that whereas Stephen Dedalus, Quentin Compson, or Mrs. Dalloway are capable of imaginatively questioning and exploring themselves and their worlds with much verbal virtuosity, Studs for the most part resists disturbing new ideas or experiences and reflects principally the values, goals, and language of his immediate culture.

Nowhere in *Studs Lonigan* is Farrell's attempt to involve us in Studs' inner life through indirect discourse more central and powerful than in Studs' feelings about sex and love. It is in Studs' thoughts and emotions about this range of experience that we come to know fully the meaning and tragedy of his life. We come to know, that is, of Studs' need for emotional communion, of his lifelong repression of this need, and of his substitution of street-culture roles for his essential nature.

It is almost a given in Studs' world that all expression of deep personal feeling is either repressed or severely channelled, since to express one's emotions openly is both to expose potential weaknesses and to suggest a lack of aggressive manliness. Our first encounter with Studs, on the evening of his grammar school graduation, reveals this habit of mind. He has become fond of one of his teachers, Battleaxe Bertha, and after the ceremony thinks of speaking to her.

> He wanted to go up to her and say goodbye, and say that he felt her to be a pretty good sport at that, but he couldn't, because there was some goofy part of himself telling himself that he couldn't. He couldn't let himself get soft about anything, because, well, just because he wasn't the kind of a bird that got soft. He never let anyone know how he felt. (YL, 36)

At fourteen, however, Studs is still not fully confirmed in his role of toughness; he still wavers during this phase of his early adolescence between his desire to share his feelings and his fear of stepping outside a group-sanctioned role. That summer, for example, in the long afternoon with Lucy in Washington Park, he responds to the peace and beauty of the park and to Lucy at his side and has what he himself realizes are a series of poetic insights into the wonder and pleasure of natural beauty and of love. He has what we might call an epiphany, and he wishes to share it with Lucy.

> He wanted to let her know about all the dissolving, tingling feelings he was having, and how he felt like he might be the lagoon, and the feelings she made inside of him were

like the dancing feelings and the little waves the sun and wind made on it; but those were things he didn't know how to tell her, and he was afraid to, because maybe he would spoil them if he did. He couldn't even say a damn thing about how it all made him want to feel strong and good, and made him want to do things and be big and brave for her. (YL, 114)

When Studs' street world discovers and ridicules this adolescent romance, he resolves to be more careful:

He liked Lucy. He liked her. He loved her, but after what had happened he was even ashamed to admit it to himself. He was a hard-boiled guy, and he had learned his lesson. He'd keep himself roped in tight after this when it came to girls. He wasn't going to show his cards to nobody again. (YL, 124)

Studs dismisses Lucy but he cannot rid himself of thinking about her, and he does so for the remainder of his life in moments of reverie. Lucy and the afternoon in the park recur again and again in Studs' consciousness not merely because they represent nostalgia for an idyllic moment in the past but because they symbolize a life of feeling which though rejected and repressed is still intensely needed and longed for.

Studs seemingly has a chance to recover Lucy—and thus recover part of himself—when, in his early twenties, he and Lucy have a date. Again a kind of epiphany combining nature, love, and the moment occurs, and again Studs is incapable of expressing himself:

It was like a picture that Studs wanted never to forget. The warm spring evening, the promise it offered to him, a mist in the lush air, Sheridan Road ahead, with traffic lights, people crossing the street, automobiles going by, the Victrola, Lucy singing, so pretty that he wanted to look at her, touch her, kiss her, love her, take her arm, say something to her of what it all meant, and of how all along he had really wanted nothing like he had wanted her. And he couldn't say anything, because it all stopped him. He guessed that when

you felt like he did, you just had too many feelings to tell
them to anybody. (YM, 277–78)

Unable to express what he feels, Studs slips unthinkingly into the
form of expression with girls which is now habitually his. He at-
tacks Lucy in the cab; she repulses him; and their relationship is
permanently ended. But there is still the need. In the long New
Year's Eve section which concludes *The Young Manhood of Studs Lonigan*, Studs gets drunk and longs for Lucy. The incident summa-
rizes the history of the relationship between Studs' inner need and
outer expression. Now as always that which Studs refuses to accept
within himself is transformed in expression into the squalid and
filthy.

> Studs staggered, and draped his arms tightly around a
> lamppost. He vomited.
> "I'm sick. I want Lucy. I love Lucy. I want Lucy. I want
> Lucy," he cried aloud, a large tear splattered on his cheek.
> The vomiting caused a violent contraction and pressure, as
> if a hammer were in his head.
> "I'm so sick! Lucy, please love Studs!" he cried.
> A light flurry of snow commenced. Studs tenderly kissed
> the cold lamppost, which suddenly seemed to be Lucy.
> "I've always loved you, Lucy!"
> Tears rolled down his drunken, dirty face. (YM, 395)

In *Judgment Day* Studs still occasionally has periods of "softness,"
usually in conjunction with moments of peace in nature. But for
the most part he feels alone and deserted, and his frustrated need
to share the worries brought on by his illness and the depression
increases these feelings. He tentatively thinks of opening himself
to his sister Frances or to his father—the members of his family he
has been closest to—but does not because (in a key word now in
Studs' life) he discovers that he is a stranger to them, as they are
strangers to him. He makes the same discovery about Catherine:

> After all, he was really a stranger to her. He was really a
> stranger to everyone else in the world also, and they really
> did not know what went on inside of him, and how he felt
> about many, many things. He wasn't sure he would want to

live so intimately with anyone as he would have to do with Catherine if he married her. (JD, 26)

Toward the end of *Judgment Day*, Studs sits on a beach with Catherine, who is now pregnant:

> He . . . asked himself how . . . did it come about that he was marrying Catherine when she seemed to him suddenly like a stranger he could never know. And that a child of his was, at this very minute, growing inside of her. He scratched his puzzled head. He felt alone, so completely alone that it seemed as if there were no one near him. All these people, too, strangers. He closed his eyes and held in his mind the naked image of Catherine, and he imagined her with him in that act that was supposed to make a guy and a girl so close, and still she seemed a stranger, and he still felt all alone. His thoughts and feelings were padlocked, completely padlocked in his mind, and when he talked, most of the time, instead of expressing them he was using words to prevent himself from letting them out, fooling people by putting into their minds a picture of himself that was not at all Studs Lonigan. (JD, 334–35)

A locked mind and feelings, projecting out into the world false images of self which make all strangers—such is Studs' final realization of himself and of the road he has traveled, rendered in an almost poetic passage of indirect discourse. In the image of E. M. Forster, Studs has failed to connect. Our recognition, through Farrell's technique of indirect discourse, of the depth and strength of his need to do so lends a tragic intensity to his failure.

Studs' inability to express his basic nature and share his deepest feelings has a distinctive 1930s cast. I can perhaps best describe this quality by comparing *Studs Lonigan* with *Winesburg, Ohio* and *Ulysses*, two 1920s novels which also deal with the inarticulate felt life. One of the significant similarities among the three works is the importance of a moment of epiphany in the lives of their central figures. In each of the novels, a character has a semi-mystical insight into his relation to the nature of things, and in each he seeks to share this vision with someone else. However, there is a difference among the three novels both in the placing of the major epiphany and in the success of the character in expressing and shar-

ing his vision. In *Winesburg* and *Ulysses*, the moment occurs toward
the end of the novel—George Willard and Helen White holding
hands in the stands at the Fair Grounds in the story "Sophistication," Bloom and Stephen together in Bloom's garden on a warm
June night after their long separate wanderings during the day—
and in both instances there is connection. In *Studs Lonigan*, however, Studs and Lucy sit in the tree in Washington Park at the opening of the novel, and Studs is incapable of reaching out to express
and share with Lucy his emotional exaltation and understanding.
Ulysses and *Winesburg* thus suggest the possibility of struggling
through to at least a temporary connection as understanding and
need grow in experience; *Studs Lonigan* suggests that experience
only increases the isolation of the spirit, that the lives of even those
of us who have the potential to share and thus make fruitful their
deepest feelings are often lives of tragic waste.

Studs' understanding of the nature of his fall—the equivalent of
the act of "discovery" in formal tragedy—emerges as a major
theme in *Studs Lonigan* in the later portions of *The Young Manhood
of Studs Lonigan*. At first the theme takes the shape of Studs'
vaguely defined discontent with his life. Working for his father as
a house painter, he centers most of his attention on the poolroom
gang and its activities but finds that these engage him less and less.
His is a mood of quiet desperation, of a sense of emptiness but of
unawareness of either the source or resolution of his discontent.
"Goddamn it, yes, there was something more to life," he says at
several points (YM, 158–59).[17] Unequipped and unwilling to examine himself closely, he seizes upon "reform" as an answer to his
malaise. If he will lead a "clean" life in body and soul, he will be
happier. He responds to Father Shannon's crusade, joins a church
youth organization, gives up the poolroom gang, and begins a regi-
men of body building at the YMCA. But these of course do not
satisfy him, and he soon falls back into the familiar round of gang
activities which climax at the New Year's Eve party.

In *Judgment Day*, the theme of awareness shifts direction and becomes more central. If *Young Lonigan* is about a boy who falls into
error and does not even realize that he has done so, and if *The
Young Manhood of Studs Lonigan* is about a young man who realizes
that something has gone wrong but is unable to understand either
the cause or the solution of his condition, *Judgment Day* is about a

prematurely burdened man who knows the mistakes he has made but is unable to prevent their consequences. *Judgment Day* thus includes a powerful thread of tragic irony. Studs in the earlier novels of the trilogy had lacked a sympathetic understanding of the needs of others and a recognition of the complexity of human nature and experience. He now begins to gain these but nevertheless cannot reverse the direction of his life. Put another way, he begins to mature too late to prevent the damage caused by his earlier immaturity but his growth nevertheless increases our involvement in his fall.

Of course, Studs is not completely transformed in *Judgment Day*. The old role-playing Studs still often surfaces, particularly in the running motif of his investment in the stock market, in which he sees himself as "a gambler, a chance-taking fool prepared to face the risk of losing all the money he had saved for years and to drop it with a game smile on his face" (JD, 71). But this familiar hard-boiled role is far less central in *Judgment Day* than the sympathetic and understanding Studs we encounter in his relations with Catherine. The centrality of Catherine in Studs' life is maintained in part by the return of the trilogy in *Judgment Day* to the form of *Young Lonigan*. *The Young Manhood of Studs Lonigan* is largely panoramic in form. It covers over twelve years, is for the most part plotless, and is dominated by lengthy accounts of disconnected moments and scenes in Studs' experience—Armistice Day, the poolroom, the New Year's Eve party—in which Farrell's intent is principally to render the chaotic lack of direction in Studs' life. *Young Lonigan* and *Judgment Day*, however, are more compact in time (about six months for each) and in theme and plot. Each is dominated by a major contrast which supplies the novel with its coherence—Weary and Lucy in *Young Lonigan*, the Imbray stock gamble and Catherine in *Judgment Day*. But whereas in *Young Lonigan* the victory is to the values represented by Weary, in *Judgment Day* the tragically ironic victory is to Lucy's surrogate Catherine.

Catherine, of course, is not Lucy in several senses, most of all in that the adolescent Studs who out of his longings and needs created an avatar of spirituality in an average teenager is now the jaded and embittered Studs who sees Catherine for what she is—a good-hearted but unremarkable young woman. Yet his clear-eyed understanding of Catherine is far more complex and rewarding than had been his adoration of Lucy. Studs with Catherine is still in part the Studs of the first two novels of the trilogy. He is as inarticulate with Catherine as he had been with Lucy (the "stranger" motif), and he also often finds Catherine lacking in comparison with his recollection of Lucy. But he has also begun to think about Catherine and to act toward her in ways which constitute the living fact (rather than the idealized impossibility) of the values which Lucy represented.

The unconscious movement of Studs toward the "connection" of identification with the feelings and needs of others is revealed most fully when he and Catherine quarrel. Studs' first impulse is to act as he had when he and Lucy had fallen out after the public blazoning of their "romance"—to adopt the tough guy role of waiting for the girl to make the first move toward reconciliation. But though

> he had won the quarrel by leaving her alone at night, sobbing in the street [,] . . . it was a victory which now impressed him as not having been worth the winning. He could tell anyone about it, and stand before them as one who hadn't backed down, or taken any crap. And he liked the idea of people seeing him as that kind of guy. And yet, he had to pay the cost of it now, he had to think of her crying, walking home alone, never seeing her again. That was an idea he didn't like so well. (JD, 204–5)

The issue is clearly joined for Studs in this passage—social pride, what others might think of him, struggles against his private recognition of the pain he has caused someone else. His new maturity is measured by his ability both to realize the feelings of others and to act as a result of that realization. He takes the initiative in making up with Catherine, and in their love-making which follows he again exhibits his growth. Rather than boasting of his conquest, he feels for the first time in sex a responsibility for what he has asked of Catherine and what she has given him. Occasionally in his relations with Catherine from this point the old Studs flares up, the Studs who wants to flaunt his toughness and discard his commitments. But for the most part he now displays in his actions toward Catherine the qualities of emotion and spirit which he had always suppressed except in his dream reveries of Lucy. After he and Catherine become lovers, he recalls his failing health and has a vision of Catherine weeping over his dead body. "God, that couldn't happen," he thinks. "It wouldn't. He had to live for her, and for himself. . . . He was beginning to see some of the things that love was. This was one" (JD, 275). He is, as before, still "afraid of himself, of the feeling of love and tenderness toward her" (JD, 277), but he is in fact thinking and acting with love and tenderness.

Studs' greater sensitivity toward others (or, in another sense, his recognition of a world of feeling outside of himself) is accompanied by a parallel sensitivity to the larger scheme of things of which he is a part. And this "scheme" in depression America is principally that of the American economic system, in which the individual is both insignificant and powerless. The Studs who in the 1920s had a fully-developed and confident sense of his own importance now thinks, "Hell, what right did he have to expect to get anywhere with all these millions and millions in the same game, with fellows starting out with dough and an education, and better health than he had? He felt small" (JD, 195).

Studs' economic and social "smallness"—and that of his father as a representative middle class American—becomes a key theme in *Judgment Day*, one closely related to the theme of tragic ignorance in the trilogy as a whole. Studs in his personal life and his father in his business life are parallel examples of the fatal consequences of blindness, of closed ideas and values. Mr. Lonigan, with his belief in hard work, good "contacts," and the responsibility of "foreigners" and international Jewish bankers for all economic problems, illustrates, in Farrell's view, the kind of blind faith in the just operation of the capitalistic system which helped precipitate and prolong the depression. Full of platitudes and prejudices about the economic and social world in which he functions, he observes with disbelief the bank runs and business failures which follow the steep decline of the stock market. His own business failure is thus analogous to Studs' physical decline after New Year's Day 1929. Both have their roots in the blindness and pride of selfishness, of a "good time" or "success" without thought of consequences. Both failures, in short, are at heart ethical failures and are thus portrayed by Farrell, at their climaxes, by the physically repugnant—in Studs drowning in his own fluid while his despairing father, who has just witnessed the final collapse of his business, sits drunkenly in the kitchen.

Yet there is an important difference between Mr. Lonigan and Studs at the close of the trilogy, a difference which stems from the persistence of the allegorical mode in the presentation of Mr. Lonigan and the greater role in *Judgment Day* of the tragic mode in the

depiction of Studs. Mr. Lonigan, because his career as a businessman encapsulates an allegory of American business life in the
twentieth century, cannot accept responsibility for his condition as
a victim of the depression. "It wasn't right nor fair," he thinks.
"What had he done . . . ? Here he was, a man who had always done
his duties" (JD, 424). But Studs, as he wanders in despairing ill
health looking for a job, realizes that the emptiness and failure of
his life are in part his responsibility. "He wished, with a weak will,
that many things that had been done could be undone" (JD,
382).[18]

One way of describing Studs as a tragic figure at the conclusion
of *Studs Lonigan* is to compare him with Clyde Griffiths at the end
of *An American Tragedy*. Both Clyde and Studs are imprisoned or
trapped toward the end of their lives—Clyde literally so in prison,
Studs metaphorically so by ill health, joblessness, and a pregnant
sweetheart. Studs himself recognizes his condition when he and
Catherine spend a day at the beach. "He looked around the beach,
as if looking though the bars of a cage, and he saw all these people
in swimming suits, so many girls, so many fellows, and he won-
dered how many of them were trapped as he was, or would be
trapped in the same way?" (JD, 330). Both figures have helped
create their own prisons because of their lack of strength and insight, but they have also been imprisoned by the narrowness of
belief and value in their worlds. Both have grown in understanding, but they find that they still cannot satisfactorily explain themselves to others and are thus still superficially judged by others. So
as "strangers" they are condemned for their past errors and go to
their deaths. In both instances, their mothers remain behind as
striking examples of failures in sympathetic understanding. The
narrow religiosity and superficial moralism of both Mrs. Griffiths
and Mrs. Lonigan (Mrs. Lonigan, revealed in her cruel treament
of Catherine) represent the persistence and continuing strength of
those aspects of life which helped seal the fate of their sons. So
both novels end on a note of deep pathos rather than of triumphant reestablishment of the moral order, as in a conventional
tragedy. Clyde and Studs have matured in understanding and feeling, but their growth has aided neither their ability to communicate with their worlds nor the moral maturity of their worlds.
Knowledge is not power; it is only the tragic consequence of experience.

John Dos Passos

U.S.A.

Criticism of Dos Passos' fiction is often colored by the naive transparency of the Dos Passos we know through his essays, reminiscences, and letters.[1] Here is a man, it seems, who came to writing in the years after World War I armed with a few conventional ideas of his day, who during the 1920s gathered up and used, like a literary magpie, the principal avant garde techniques of the period, and who produced a series of historically significant but imaginatively deficient works culminating in *U.S.A.*, after which his work settled into the permanent dullness which best reflects his fundamental mediocrity.

There is some truth to this estimate of Dos Passos and his work. From his early Harvard essays to his late fiction he was preoccupied with the theme of the conflict between the Sensitive Young Man and a mechanistic world and with the related subject of the dangers to individual freedom posed by modern political and social institutions.[2] He seems never, in other words, to have advanced in ideas beyond his early absorption in Joyce's *Portrait of the Artist as a Young Man* (which he read twice before the end of the war)[3] and his acceptance of his father's late nineteenth century Spencerian version of Jeffersonian individualism.[4] In both frames of reference, the person seeking to preserve freedom of feeling and action is good; the world outside is crass and restrictive and thus ultimately destructive and evil. By the late 1920s, after a decade of interest and experimentation in avant garde fiction, drama, poetry, and film, Dos Passos found a suitable form for the expression of these conventional ideas. Joycean stream-of-consciousness and narrative discontinuity, German expressionistic drama and film, impressionistic biography, experimental free verse—these and still other twenties enthusiasms helped chart his development from the comparatively conventional form of *Three Soldiers* in 1921 to the experimental techniques of *U.S.A.* in the early 1930s. *U.S.A.* is thus assumed to be a novel in which a 1930s naturalistic intensification of a traditional romantic theme—the oppressive nature of the world—is communicated in several fashionable experimental modes. Our interest in the novel is therefore in its form as a panoramic social novel. Otherwise, we are led to believe, the narrative portions are flat and dull, the newsreels obvious, and the Camera Eye obscure; only the biographies, because of their mordant satire, are of permanent interest.

This is, I think, a fair account of the conventional estimate of Dos Passos' work and of *U.S.A.* in particular. Yet many readers have found that *U.S.A.* has a holding power—the power to drive one to the conclusion of an extremely long book—which they associate with the greatest fiction. They are absorbed in its characters and events because these seem to communicate something moving about human nature and experience, not because the trilogy documents easily grasped ideas in fashionably experimental forms. Their response to *U.S.A.* as a work of fullness and depth suggests that the trilogy is not a collection of fragments but rather a powerful and complex unity—a unity which I propose to describe as that of a naturalistic tragedy.

The surface impression of *U.S.A.*, however, is indeed of miscellaneousness. The three novels—*The 42nd Parallel* (1930), *Nineteen Nineteen* (1934), and *The Big Money* (1936)—contain twelve discontinuous fictional narratives (in effect twelve different plots), twenty-seven brief biographies of famous late nineteenth- and early twentieth-century Americans, sixty-eight newsreels consisting of snippets from popular songs and newspaper headlines and stories, and fifty-one Camera Eye passages which use modified stream-of-consciousness material to render specific moments in the inner life of the author from his youth to the early 1930s. In addition, each of the novels has a distinctive subject matter. Mac dominates *The 42nd Parallel*, Joe Williams and Richard Savage *Nineteen Nineteen*, and Charley Anderson and Margo Williams *The Big Money*, while the setting shifts in emphasis from small-town America in the first volume to Paris and Rome in *Nineteen Nineteen* to New York in the final novel.

Of course, there is a correspondingly superficial unity to this diversity of subject matter and form in that the trilogy (as most critics have observed) is a parody epic. The histories of twelve Americans of various backgrounds and occupations but of similarly unsatisfactory lives is a 1930s version of the twelve books or cantos devoted to the career of an epic hero. Epics demand the inclusion of much material involving the heroic past of the nation or race, and *U.S.A.* is therefore also a historical novel. The major political and cultural figures of the age are the subject of the biographies and several also appear in the narratives (Wilson, Bryan, and Big Bill Haywood, for example). A number of fictional figures are based on recognizable historical personages (the publicist Ivy Lee served as a model for J. Ward Moorehouse, as did Bernarr Macfadden for Doc Bingham).[5] The principal events of American life from approximately 1900 to 1931 figure prominently in all of *U.S.A.* and not merely in the newsreels. By "events" I mean not only such specific historical occasions as the outbreak of war or the Sacco and Vanzetti executions but such phenomena as Prohibition, political and labor radicalism, the Florida land boom, the rise of the aircraft industry and of Hollywood, and so on. We come to know, too, a great deal about such American cities as Chicago, New York, Washington, Philadelphia, Pittsburgh, and Los Angeles. The career of each fictional character therefore renders not only a representative type of modern American (the public relations man, the inventor-entrepreneur, the IWW radical) but a representative range of historical and social life. *U.S.A.* thus appears to be largely an obvious exercise in imitative form, in which the theme of the discontinuity, fragmentation, and miscellaneousness of American life is both epic theme and form.

Yet there is much in *U.S.A.* which conflicts with this seemingly inevitable conclusion and which suggests that we must look further and deeper for a full understanding of the relation of theme to form in the trilogy. For example, fictional characters frequently appear in narratives other than their own (a device I shall call "interlacing"), and specific historical events frequently control an entire group of narratives, biographies, newsreels, and Camera Eye segments in a particular portion of the novel (a device I shall call "cross-stitching").

Interlacing occurs in a number of ways in *U.S.A.* Minor figures, for example, reappear in the narratives of several different major characters. (By "major character" I mean one of the twelve figures who have narratives devoted to them.) Doc Bingham in a sense frames the trilogy by his appearance in the opening narrative devoted to Mac and his reappearance at the close of *The Big Money* as a client of Moorehouse's advertising firm, while the labor faker George W. Barrow and the newspapermen Jerry Burnham and

Don Stevens reappear frequently throughout the trilogy. Love affairs occur between a number of major figures and thus create a frequent interlacing effect. Among the most prominent of such relationships are Daughter and Dick Savage, Dick and Eveline, Moorehouse and Eveline, Moorehouse and Eleanor, Charley and Eveline, and Mary French and Ben Compton. J. Ward Moorehouse in particular pervades the trilogy in an interlacing role. He is an important figure in the narratives of Eleanor, Janey, Eveline, and Dick Savage, and he appears occasionally or is mentioned in those of Mac, Joe Williams, and Daughter. On two notable occasions (an evening in a Paris nightclub during the war, and a New York party in the late 1920s) four or five of the major characters are briefly interlaced. Occasionally there is a sense of forcing when two characters are interlaced under unlikely circumstances, as when Dick and Joe meet briefly in Genoa or when Mac learns of Moorehouse's presence in Mexico City. But in general the effect is curiously appropriate—curious because of the range of life surveyed in the trilogy, appropriate because the intertwining of the lives of so many diverse figures seems to confirm our feeling that there is a rich substrata of relatedness to their experience.

Cross-stitching occurs most obviously when a new major character and thus a new area of experience is introduced. So the initial appearance of Margo, who is to become a Hollywood star, is accompanied by biographies of Isadora Duncan and Valentino, much newsreel reporting of Hollywood high jinks, and the presence of the Camera Eye in New York art life. The inventor Charley Anderson and the radical Ben Compton have similar cross-stitched introductions. A second kind of cross-stitching consists of the frequent reappearance of a major social phenomenon in a number of narratives as well as in various biographies, newsreels and Camera Eye segments. The IWW-led strike, the stock market boom, and Greenwich Village art life are a few examples. The war, above all, is present in the trilogy as an event touching almost everyone. Of all the major figures, only Mac (who retreats to Mexico before it begins) and Mary French and Margo (who are too young) are not in some significant way involved in the war. And the war dominates the newsreels, many of the biographies, and much of the Camera Eye of *Nineteen Nineteen* as well as major portions of the other two novels.

Through the interlacing of characters and cross-stitching of events Dos Passos appears to be saying that though we seem to be a nation of separate strands, we are in fact intertwined in a fabric of relatedness. Dos Passos was seeking, in short, to create a symbolic form to express the theme that though we lead many different lives in a multiplicity of experience, these lives are part of our shared national life; thus our meaning as individuals and as a nation lies in the meaning which arises out of the inseparable unity of individual lives and national character.

Dos Passos provides an introduction to this meaning in his comment that the basic theme of all his work is "man's struggle for life against the strangling institutions he himself creates."[6] What lends distinction and vitality to his fictional rendering of this conventional Jeffersonian concept is his ability to dramatize our life-denying institutions as the ideas, beliefs, and values which we unconsciously and habitually express in our thoughts and feelings and thus in our language. His method is both verbal (in the sense of the language people use) and ironic. Dos Passos has claimed that the novelist is "the historian of the age he lives in,"[7] but he has also noted that "the mind of a generation is its speech,"[8] and he concluded the opening sketch of his trilogy, the sketch itself entitled "U.S.A.," with the comment that "mostly U.S.A. is the speech of the people."[9] When Carl Sandburg, in 1936, sought in his book-length poem *The People, Yes* to express the same belief, he celebrated the innate wisdom and courage of the folk which are embodied in their language. Dos Passos, on the other hand, suggested by the powerful ironic current in his dramatization of "the voice of the people" that the language of democratic idealism in America, because it disguises various suspect values, subverts the very ideals this language purports to express and reflects instead a deep malaise at the heart of American life.

As several of Dos Passos' best critics have sensed, *U.S.A.* is a novel in which most of the conventional attributes of fiction—plot, character, setting, and symbol—are subordinated to a vast and complex exercise in verbal irony.[10] The narratives in *U.S.A.*, both because of their relative length within the trilogy as a whole and because of the inherent nature of narrative, are the fullest expression of Dos Passos' ironic method. His technique is to use a version of indirect discourse to reveal the underlying nature of his narrative figures and thus to reveal as well the important similarities among these figures.

In response to a question asked in 1965 about the source of his technique of indirect discourse, Dos Passos replied that he was uncertain but that he believed he may have derived it from Zola and Joyce.[11] If so, he modified his own practice greatly, since his indirect discourse lacks both the slangy raciness of Zola (or Farrell) and the disconnected flux of Joyce. Instead, Dos Passos suggests by a number of devices that it is the very texture of his narrative prose—its vocabulary and syntax as a whole—which reflects a character's habitual modes of thought and expression. The narratives in *U.S.A.* contain remarkably little dialogue or dramatic scene because the author's narrative voice is itself essentially a dramatic rendering of character.

Dos Passos supplies several verbal keys to remind us occasionally that we are reading the author's rhetorical reshaping of a character's habitual voice. One is to place eye-catching colloquialisms in his third-person prose ("ud" for "would," for example), another is to run together as single words phrases that are spoken as single words ("officeboy," for example). A third is to open a narrative which depicts the childhood of a character in a prose style which is obviously childlike. Here, for example, is most of the first paragraph of Eveline Hutchins' narrative:

> Little Eveline and Arget and Lade and Gogo lived on the top floor of a yellowbrick house on the North Shore Drive. Arget and Lade were little Eveline's sisters. Gogo was her little brother littler than Eveline; he had such nice blue eyes but Miss Mathilda had horrid blue eyes. On the floor below was Dr. Hutchins' study where Yourfather mustn't be disturbed, and Dearmother's room where she stayed all morning painting dressed in a lavender smock. On the groundfloor was the drawingroom and the diningroom, where parishioners came and little children must be seen and not heard, and at dinnertime you could smell good things to eat and hear knives and forks and tinkly companyvoices and Yourfather's booming scary voice. . . . (NN, 107)

The irony in this passage is readily apparent but gentle. Far more characteristic of Dos Passos' use of indirect discourse for ironic effect are the many occasions in the narrative when a character's thoughts are rendered in a blatantly clichéd verbal style which clearly reflects the painful inadequacy of his stereotyped beliefs. So, for example, when Joe Williams is arrested in wartime Liverpool for drunkenness, Dos Passos' account of the magistrate's lecture to him and his comrades captures both Joe's colloquial idiom and the magistrate's hackneyed jingoism.

> And the magistrate in the little wig gave 'em a hell of a talking to about how this was wartime and they had no right being drunk and disorderly on British soil but had ought to be fighting shoulder to shoulder with their brothers, Englishmen of their own blood and to whom the Americans owed everything, even their existence as a great nation, to defend civilization and free institutions and plucky little Belgium against the invading huns who were raping women and sinking peaceful merchantmen. (NN, 45)

Somewhat different in technique, but similar in effect in reminding us that Dos Passos is engaging us in the minds of his characters through their verbal formulas, is the passage reporting J. Ward Moorehouse's thoughts when he discovers that the rich man's daughter he had hoped to marry has been sleeping with a Frenchman. Here it is the last phrase which brings us up short.

> He walked down the street without seeing anything. For a while he thought he'd go down to the station and take the first train out and throw the whole business to ballyhack, but there was the booklet to get out, and there was a chance that if the boom did come he might get in on the ground floor, and this connection with money and the Strangs; opportunity knocks but once at a young man's door. (FP, 193)

In fact, however, the narrative prose style in *U.S.A.* is generally far less blatant than these examples in its indirect-discourse rendering of the platitudes and clichés which guide the lives of the characters. Rather, Dos Passos' more common method is to suggest by the jaded, worn, and often superficially flat language of the narratives the underlying failure of understanding of those who approach life without independent vision and who are therefore "strangled" by the hold of the conventional upon their minds. And yet—and this is the source of the strength of the narratives as satiric fiction—this pervasive flatness is subtly and often powerfully ironic, since it always points to some specific limitation in the character depicted. Here, for example, is a typical passage of narrative prose, one in which without any bold ironic touches Dos Passos describes Janey Williams' new position as secretary in a Washington law office just before America's entrance into the war.

> Working at Dreyfus and Carroll's was quite different from working at Mrs. Robinson's. There were mostly men in the office. Mr. Dreyfus was a small thinfaced man with a small black moustache and small black twinkly eyes and a touch of accent that gave him a distinguished foreign diplomat manner. He carried yellow wash gloves and a yellow cane and had a great variety of very much tailored overcoats. He was the brains of the firm, Jerry Burnham said. Mr. Carroll was a stout redfaced man who smoked many cigars and cleared his throat a great deal and had a very oldtimey Southern Godblessmysoul way of talking. Jerry Burnham said he was the firm's bay window. Jerry Burnham was a wrinklefaced young man with dissipated eyes who was the firm's adviser in technical and engineering matters. He laughed a great deal, always got into the office late, and for some reason took a fancy to Janey and used to joke about things to her while he was dictating. She liked him, though the dissipated look under his eyes scared her off a little. She'd have liked to have talked to him like a sister, and gotten him to stop burning the candle at both ends. (FP, 152)

On the one hand, the passage merely records Janey's impressions of the various members of the firm and thus renders in a mildly ironic manner several of her received opinions: that fine clothes represent distinction, that speech mannerisms signify character, and that there are clear physical stigmata of moral decay—in short, that life is as superficially apparent as she finds it. But the passage also records, with a far deeper and more significant irony, Janey's unconscious absorption in Jerry Burnham and her fear of that absorption, a conflict which she seeks to resolve by her adoption of the role of "sister" toward him. Janey thus reveals in the seemingly bland prose of this passage her fear of her own emotions and desires, a fear which leads her to erect barriers of conventional and life-denying attitudes and roles between herself and the world.

Each of the narratives in *U.S.A.* demonstrates that its major character is locked in an analogous prison of stereotyped thought and action which is reflected in his language. Although indirect discourse with an ironic thrust is the pervasive mode of the narratives, Dos Passos combines with this technique the equally ironic devices of the verbal motif and the paradigmatic action, devices which also enforce the theme that most Americans live unexamined lives within closed systems of belief. The verbal motif is a word or phrase habitual to a character's thought or speech which defines the character's response to experience, and the paradigmatic action occurs early in a character's life and then reappears again and again in various guises. Both the motif and the action are unconscious and repetitious; they create a safe and comforting enclosure of feeling and thought from which a character can maneuver without undertaking disturbing explorations of himself or of experience.

In *U.S.A.* characters do not develop or change in relation to experience, as in a conventional novel of character and plot. Rather, characters remain static and what changes in the course of time and the occurrence of major events are the patterns of failure within the American system. It is not our understanding of the characters which is filled out but our understanding of the nature of the nation as a whole. Dos Passos substitutes a number of developing thematic similarities among the narrative characters for the more conventional device of individual character development. It is therefore necessary to say something initially about each of the major characters, emphasizing the verbal motif or paradigmatic action which helps define his static nature, before going on to the patterns which emerge out of the narratives as a whole.

Mac's character is defined in his adolescence when he takes a job with the book salesman Doc Bingham. He soon realizes that Bingham is a charlatan but decides to remain with him. "Anyway, it was a job" (FP, 38), he says resignedly. Although Mac acquires radical ideas from his reading and experience, he is constantly betrayed in the expression of these ideas by his weakness of will. He is betrayed above all, in a kind of Marxist allegory, by the bourgeois comforts of a wife, a home, and a business. In the last segment devoted to him we leave him worrying about his property during the furor of the Mexican revolution.

Janey is born into the genteel restrictions of a Southern lower middle class world. Early in life, in the incident of her friendship with a black girl, she learns that she is expected to suppress natural feeling for the sake of propriety. She eventually attaches herself, a washed-out spinster, to Moore-house, who represents to her both a paternal wisdom and authority and a safe masculinity.

Moorehouse reveals his unchanging basic character when as a youth he unconsciously exploits his thirty-five year old piano teacher and then departs without a word. Through-out his life Moorehouse will use to good advantage his in-gratiating openness and seeming idealism. He will in par-ticular rely on the term "cooperation" to represent his belief that men of opposing views—industry and labor, for ex-ample—can work together if they come to understand each other better under his guidance. But in fact Moorehouse never examines either his own motives or his verbiage and thus blandly and profitably exploits the gullible throughout his life.

Eleanor, whose father is a clerk in the Chicago stockyards, has learned to take refuge in art from the "animal" in life. "Art was something ivory white and very pure and noble and distant and sad" (FP, 211). "Refined" is her verbal motif, and she uses its suggestion of an aesthetic sensibility to con-ceal both her emotional sterility and her calculating use of others.

Charley Anderson is "only a mechanic," as he says repeat-edly when he wishes to identify something worthy and pro-ductive in his nature despite his pursuit of the big money. His childhood poverty has led him to identify the good life and freedom with wealth. But in truth he remains "only a mechanic" in that his underlying naiveté and openness make him an easy target in worlds where shrewdness and deception are required to survive. His essential weakness is revealed in early manhood when a friend gets Charley's girl-friend pregnant while he is in the hospital, and it is later revealed again and again in business deals and love relation-ships in which friends, associates, financées, and wives de-ceive him.

Eveline is an upper middle class girl (her father is a suc-cessful clergyman) who is over-protected from experience. She therefore craves it but despite her open emotional na-ture cannot understand what she wants. She cultivates a

manner of aloofness—life is "interesting" or "tiresome"—
but in fact is desperately seeking an emotional center. So
her life is a series of disastrous love affairs culminating in a
"rebound" marriage and suicide.

Joe Williams, Janey's brother, rebels against the restrictive
roles she accepts and runs away to become a seaman. We
first encounter him when he has just deserted from the navy
and is being cheated in the purchase of forged able-bodied
seaman papers. In incident after incident which follows, officials and woman take advantage of him wherever he travels. He is forever the good-natured but dull-minded butt of
the shrewd and unscrupulous, and he dies in an inconse-
quential bar brawl in St. Nazaire.

Richard Ellsworth Savage learns early in life that "gentle-
manly manners," family connections, and good looks can
carry him far. But he also learns from his early affair with a
minister's sexually repressed wife that his upper middle
class world requires the disguise or suppression of his deepest feelings. Although he thinks of himself at Harvard and
during the war as an artist and a rebel, he is in fact striving
to make himself acceptable and pleasing. His rebelliousness
fails the test offered by the war, and he drifts into the role
of Moorehouse's subordinate and eventual successor.

Daughter (perhaps the least satisfactorily characterized
major figure in *U.S.A.*) has grown up in a man-dominated
Texas world and views herself as a creature to be admired
and petted. Her entire life is focused on her need to be
loved, and when she is rejected (when pregnant) by Dick
Savage, she reaches out for and finds death in an airplane
accident.

Ben Compton, a Brooklyn Jew, laces his speech with the
catch phrases of the radical left. He has an almost religious
faith in Marxist ideology, a faith which lends him dignity
and courage (as well as an occasional ludicrousness) but
which also results in his dismissal from the Communist
Party because of his refusal to follow the party line.

As a child Mary French resented her ambitious and genteel mother and identified with her father, an over-worked
and self-sacrificing physician. After a few years at college,
she drifts into social work and then radical activities, but her
commitment to the left has the non-ideological, personal

character of her earlier family relationships. Because she is loyal to friends and true to what she knows at first hand, she constantly suffers in a movement characterized by personal betrayal and ideological conformity.

Margo is a pretty child who is raped by her step-father. She makes her way through life viewing men as untrustworthy but exploitable. Toughened by experience, her rise to stardom in Hollywood also reveals her picaresque qualities of piquant good humor, sympathy for the down and out, and genial amorality.

The twelve narratives of *U.S.A.* communicate in various interlocking patterns far more subtly and powerfully than any one narrative the theme of the failure of American life. One such pattern arises out of the use of a reappearing minor character whose manifest hypocrisy finds an almost universal echo in the major figures and who thus suggests an underlying similarity in their lives. George Barrow, who appears initially in Mac's narrative in *The 42nd Parallel* and whom we last encounter in *The Big Money* as a passive observer of the Sacco-Vanzetti case, is the principal figure of this kind. Throughout the trilogy he is a symbol of the insipid betrayal of liberal and progressive ideals by a presumed defender of those ideals. In his professional career he is an agent of organized labor, and in his personal affairs an advocate of "the art of life" (his own verbal motif). But in truth he is less interested in social and personal freedom than in maintaining an even keel in rough waters. He is the minor functionary whose bland thinness of commitment to the principles he is identified with actually subverts these principles. His appearance in a narrative usually signals a turn to the easy way out by the major character in that narrative.

Doc Bingham is an even more striking barometer of falseness. He appears only twice—early in Mac's narrative in *The 42nd Parallel* as an itinerant book salesman and late in *The Big Money* as the owner of a large patent medicine company. On both occasions he is the master of the art of perverting a large truth for a small purpose. As a book salesman he claims, while selling pornography to country boys, that "My God is the truth, that rising ever higher in the hands of honest men will dispel the mists of ignorance and greed, and bring freedom and knowledge to mankind" (FP, 32). At the close of the trilogy he encourages Moorehouse and Savage to promote his worthless patent medicines by linking their consumption to the American ideals of "selfservice, independence, individualism" (BM, 494). The difference between the two occasions is of degree rather than kind. Bingham in 1900 is just another dishonest peddler in rural America; in 1929 the huge growth in the national ability to disseminate and reward falseness has made him wealthy and powerful.

The most important way in which the narratives as a group represent theme is through what I shall call narrative clusters. Some of these clusters parallel Dos Passos' interlacing device. That is, a number of major figures not only appear in each other's narratives but also have a basic similarity of character and fate. Other clusters evolve out of discrete narratives in which the major characters never mix but nevertheless share a common destiny. An example of the first kind of cluster is the group of major figures who revolve around J. Ward Moorehouse as patron or employer: Janey, Eleanor, and Dick Savage. All three are from white-collar backgrounds of minor clerks or officials and all three are intent on solidifying their position in settings of greater gentility, power, and wealth. To do so, however, requires a repression of those emotions or drives, particularly the sexual, which might jeopardize their advance. All three, at the close of the trilogy, are both successful and desperately unhappy, with the "unnaturalness" of their lives represented most of all by their sexual failures. Eleanor is frigid, Janey has channelled her sexuality into a fierce and paranoic protectiveness toward Moorehouse, and Dick refuses to acknowledge his homosexuality.

Unlike the group of figures revolving around Moorehouse, Eveline, Joe Williams, and Daughter constitute a cluster in which the characters do not interlace. (Dick Savage, however, knows or meets all three.) Eveline, Joe, and Daughter share a tragic innocence. They are "open" characters in the sense that they acknowledge their emotional (and sexual) natures and seek personal fulfillment as much as their circumstances allow. Eveline and Daughter want love, Joe freedom. But they are without strength or shrewdness, and thus for them something ventured is all lost. Daughter's openhearted love for Dick and his desertion of her despite her pregnancy suggests the similar victimization of all three figures by the more ruthless and circumspect. So all three go to bitter and meaningless deaths, victims of a naively innocent failure to realize that to desire is to make oneself vulnerable.

Mac and Joe also never interlace but have basically similar characters and fates, even though Mac's fate is bourgeois respectability and Joe's is death. Both represent the life of the working man at its most empty and futile. Until Mac moves into the middle class at the close of his narrative, their lives are of constant movement— Mac throughout America as a laborer, Joe throughout the world as a seaman. They are archetypically rootless American workingmen, in permanent transit not because they wish to be but because their marginal lives prevent them from putting down roots. And because they are marginal and thus weak, Mac and Joe are beaten up and robbed and cheated and deceived wherever they go. Both are also victimized (in a Marxist sense) by sex. They marry because girls whom they desire withhold sex as leverage to gain a husband. After marriage, their wives struggle for the possessions which signify a rise in status. So both take the road again, with their ultimate destinies—Mac sinking into a mindless desire for security, Joe dying in a bar—representing the two extremes of defeat for the workingman.

Mac is occasionally active in the IWW, and Joe, while not politically conscious, resents America's participation in the war. Both figures belong to an early phase of American radicalism. Ben Compton and Mary French, however, play active roles in the more theoretically based and institutionally structured radicalism of the 1920s. Yet both share with Mac and Joe an essential naiveté which to Dos Passos is the tragic center of modern American radicalism. Ben is a textbook Marxist and Mary is responsive to the misery she sees around her in city slums and in factory and mine towns. Both therefore lack an appreciation of the maneuvering, compromise, and betrayal which are central to left-wing radicalism after the war. So Ben is dismissed from the party as a deviationist because he fails to accept that party discipline supercedes Marxist truth, and Mary labors fruitlessly in the trenches of the movement because her political innocence is suspect.

The most significant cluster of narratives in *U.S.A.* is that of Moorehouse, Charley Anderson, and Margo Dowling as inversions of the American myth of success. Moorehouse's life is an ironic fulfillment of an Alger-like rise. Born on the Fourth of July, a reader of *Success* magazine in his youth, he works hard and "didn't drink or smoke and was keeping himself clean for the lovely girl he was going to marry, a girl in pink organdy with golden curls and a sunshade" (FP, 177). But Moorehouse's good luck in twice marrying the boss's daughter (in his two marriages) also includes having to accept sexually soiled and neurotic women who make his life a misery. And his upward-moving career—from selling real estate to public relations work for steel and oil corporations to pushing the war effort and fighting the "radical element" and finally to Madison Avenue advertising—touches upon the major areas of American life in which a false rhetoric of Americanism can be used by the wealthy and powerful to exploit the poor and weak. Moorehouse has risen by pluck and luck to eminence because he has been able to manipulate the naive faiths by which most Americans live, including their faith in the Alger myth.

Charley Anderson represents a different kind of inversion of the American success myth. He aspires to be a Henry Ford or Thomas Edison, a tinkerer of genius. A country boy come to the city, he will work hard to build a better mousetrap (an airplane engine for him) and thus rise to fame and fortune while aiding mankind through his ingenuity. But Charley soon discovers that hard work and mechanical inventiveness alone do not bring the rewards promised by the myth. In an almost allegorically precise demonstration of one of Thorstein Veblen's principal theses, he learns that ruthlessness and deception are also required. Although Charley tries to ape these qualities, his essentially trusting and open nature makes him an easy mark for more skilled corporation in-fighters. Seeking the big money, he is almost casually devoured by more rapacious birds of prey, while he himself helps destroy those who are even more naively honest and faithful than he himself—notably his old mechanic friend Bill Cermak. So Charley becomes a garrulous and drunken hulk, a corrupted Honest Workman.

Like Charley, Margo Dowling is poor and likeable, and she too discovers that success requires the perversion of one's most salable commodity—mechanical skill for Charley, sex for Margo. Her rise to stardom is a parody of the Hollywood version of the rags-to-riches career of the movie star. As in a film, poverty and hardship in youth are followed by work as a Ziegfeld girl, pursuit by a wealthy Yale halfback, obscurity in Hollywood, and at last discovery by a famous European director and marriage to her handsome leading man. In Margo's case, however, this rise is achieved not by hard work and good luck but rather by the open exploitation of her sexuality and by her ability at every stage of her rise to achieve an effective level of phoniness. In Hollywood, for example, a rented Rolls-Royce, relatives who pose as servants, and a false for-

eign background win her the entry into films that her talent could
not. And once in the door, it is only her willingness to play the
sexual games demanded by her kinky director (himself a Margo
kind of phony) and by a sexual-athlete male star which assures her
rise. Margo ends as a Jean Harlow figure—blonde, hard, shrewd,
someone who has what she wants and who accepts what she had to
do to get it.

The ironic inversion of the myth of success in the Moorehouse,
Anderson, and Margo narratives occurs as well in two other major
strands of the complex fabric which is *U.S.A.* The first is found in
the anonymous biographies at the opening, approximate middle,
and close of the trilogy—"U.S.A.," "the Body of an American," and
"Vag." The three figures recapitulate the failure of the American
dream. The "young man" of the opening sketch seeks a Whitmanesque community of shared labor and finds only loneliness and
"words telling about longago." [12] The Unknown Soldier has spilled
his blood to save the Morgan loans. And the hungry hobo who
walks the dusty road (while planes overhead carry the rich) recalls
that "books said opportunity, ads promised speed, own your home,
shine bigger than your neighbor." (BM, 561).

A second major analogue to Dos Passos' ironic portrayal of the
myth of success in the narratives occurs in his full-scale attention
in the trilogy to two of the major moments in the history of the
American consciousness in the twentieth century—the war and the
Sacco-Vanzetti case. Both events have the same configuration:
vested authority believes that it is pursuing a course of action that
is necessary to preserve American ideals, and particularly the ideal
of freedom, but in fact is aiding in the corruption and destruction
of these ideals. In both instances, the failure of the American
dream is so massively evident that this failure takes on mythic resonance. It is not merely the super-patriots and the Massachusetts
establishment who falsify the great words—democracy, freedom,
happiness—but the nation as a whole. The end of the war in *Nineteen Nineteen* and the deaths of Sacco and Vanzetti at the close of
The Big Money are thus the historical equivalents of the narratives
of Moorehouse, Anderson, and Margo. In both the historical event
and the fictional life the American dream, including the dream of
success, is not only false but is itself corrupting.

Although the biographies in *U.S.A.* appear to be radically different in theme and form from the narratives, they are in fact essen-

tially similar. Of course, the biographies substitute a stylized impressionistic selectivity for fully extended narration. But in the biographies as in the narratives the principal mode is irony. Often the very title of the biography is ironic ("Meester Veelson" or—for Carnegie—"Prince of Peace"); or, as in the narratives, a key word is used to reflect an obsession ("righteousness" for Roosevelt, "ideas" for Ford). Most of all, irony oozes out of every phrase in the biographies because they are studies in reversal of received opinion. In them, the presumed great of American life are revealed to be betrayers of American values and the conventionally vilified to be heroic and noble. I will, at this point, discuss Dos Passos' ironic portrayal of the just and successful, reserving my discussion of the other biographies until later in this chapter.

Dos Passos' biographies of the presumed great divide into clusters of analogous "life stories," clusters which offer a massive confirmation in public lives of the dramatization in the fictional narratives of the perversion of the American myth of success. There are three clusters of bitterly ironic biographies of the great in *U.S.A.*: the robber barons (Minor Keith, J. P. Morgan, and Samuel Insull); the misguided or hypocritical do-gooders (W. J. Bryan, Roosevelt, Carnegie, Wilson, and Hearst); and the callous industrialists (Frederick Taylor and Ford). Considerably less biting in tone are the biographies of a cluster of inventors and artists (Burbank, Edison, the Wright brothers, Steinmetz, Isadora Duncan, and Valentino) who, while themselves not directly culpable, have nevertheless permitted themselves or their work to be controlled by the powerful and wealthy of America. The robber barons and assembly-line industrialists—the open manipulators of the system for their own profit—are easy game for Dos Passos' irony, particularly when they display an interest in art or politics, and he dispatches them effectively. His deepest anger and longest biographies are reserved for those who have used the rhetoric of American idealism but who, in his view, have betrayed that idealism because of their class or religious bias (Roosevelt and Wilson) or ambition (Hearst). In contrast to the caustic tone of these biographies, Dos Passos' tone in his portraits of duped men and women of creative genius is more ambivalent and occasionally even sympathetic. Here the fault, as with Edison, is often of preoccupation, or, as with Valentino, of naiveté. Nevertheless, though used by the system, all—whether consciously or not—have also used the system to gain success. All are therefore portrayed ironically in that their fame as artists or inventors echoes the falseness and hollowness of the society which has rewarded them.

Since all four of these clusters of biographies are ironic success stories, they are evocatively related to the ironic success narratives of Moorehouse, Anderson, and Margo. The sanctimoniously self-righteous rhetoric of Wilson and the hypocritical "public interest" journalism of Hearst are powerful public parallels to the methods and career of J. Ward Moorehouse. Charley Anderson's life as a tinkerer is closely related to the lives of Ford, Taylor, and Edison. Like Taylor, he believes that his "responsibility to the shareholders" requires him to impose dehumanizing conditions upon his work force. But more significantly he differs from Edison and Ford (and thus gains a tragic dimension) in that he can neither retreat into his work room nor push single-mindedly toward the big money he craves. And Margo, who has been transformed into a star by the image-making capacity of Hollywood, has her analogues in Isadora Duncan and Valentino, two figures whose artificially enlarged public personalities tragically outrun their ability to fulfill them.

The newsreels in *U.S.A.* maintain the ironic technique of the trilogy as a whole. They consist of authentic snippets from contemporary headlines, news stories, speeches, and songs—contemporary in the sense that they roughly parallel the forward-moving chronology of the narratives and Camera Eye from approximately the turn of the century to the early 1930s. Their authenticity produces an immediate ironic effect, since the "real" world they depict is one of trivia and hysteria, of the significant reduced to the superficial by simplistic loading, and of the superficial bloated into importance because of its "human interest." The newsreels create an impression not of life but, as in the indirect discourse of the narratives, of life seen through a distorting lens which has failed to recognize the gap between events and the falsified language used to report them.

Like the other modes in *U.S.A.*, the newsreels contain much ironic interlacing and cross-stitching. As always, the war offers the most obvious illustrations. Newsreel XIX in *The 42nd Parallel*, for example, contains a number of items dealing with America's entrance into the war. Run between verses from the patriotic "Over There" are news items noting huge profits for the Colt Firearms Company, legislation to restrict blacks from white areas, and pleas for the punishment of "abusers" of the flag. So the inspiring lyrics about America's role in Europe are juxtaposed against the war profits, racial prejudice, and intolerant super-patriotism which the war has permitted at home. The newsreels frequently cross-stitch with the other modes, most often, of course, with the narratives, since many of the narrative figures are engaged in activities— strikes, the war, the stock market boom, etc.—which are also public news. More suggestive, however, is the cross-stitching between the newsreels and the Camera Eye, a device which reflects both the ironic disparity between public reporting and private vision and the involvement of the Camera Eye in the events and issues of his day. For example, Newsreel xxi of *Nineteen Nineteen* is largely war news, including the arrival of American troops in Europe and military successes of the Allies. It also contains passages from several jolly and humorous war songs, the most lengthy of which is "Mr. Zip," whose "hair [is] cut just as short as mine" (NN, 70). This newsreel is followed by Camera Eye 29, in which the consciousness depicted is at the front fingering his close cropped head. He hears artillery to the north "pounding the thought of death into our ears" and thinks of "the limits of the hard immortal skull under the flesh" and of "a deathshead and skeleton" which sits "wearing glasses in the arbor . . . inside the new khaki uniform inside my twentyoneyearold body" (NN, 71–72). So the superficialities of reportage and of popular song are transformed into the poetic images of personal truth.

The character of *U.S.A.* as a naturalistic tragedy derives not only from the "stranglehold" of falsified American ideals on American life and belief. If also arises from the presence in the trilogy of those who struggle through to an understanding of the corruption of the American dream and who seek to express this understanding in word and deed. This theme in *U.S.A.* appears most clearly and powerfully in the biographies and Camera Eye, though it is also obliquely present in the narratives.

Several biography clusters are devoted to the possibility of the heroic life in America—to the life dedicated to the pursuit of truth in words and action by those willing to be ignored or vilified or martyred because they run against the grain of American life established by the powerful and corrupt. One such cluster is of fallen leaders: Big Bill Haywood, Robert La Follette, and Eugene Debs. These three pre-war leaders sought to express through a radical

ideal—the IWW, progressivism, and socialism—a vision of a better
life for all Americans. Each, in the more innocent days before the
war, met with some success. But the career of each was destroyed
as old enemies exploited the super-patriotism of war hysteria to
crush all forms of liberalism. Another cluster consists of the martyred radicals, Jack Reed, Joe Hill, and Wesley Everett. Here, as in
the narratives, Dos Passos depicts pre-war radicalism more affirmatively than its post-war communist version. Reed, Hill, and
Everett are native Americans (westerners all—Reed's motif is that
he is "a westerner and words meant what they said") (NN, 14) who
seek to translate the old words into acts and who are killed or die
in the effort. And finally there is the cluster of the vilified truth-
sayers, writers and thinkers and artists such as Randolph Bourne,
Thorstein Veblen, Paxton Hibben, and Frank Lloyd Wright. These
are men who struggle to say something true about the war or eco-
nomics or diplomacy or architecture. Each, like Veblen, finds that
so much falsehood is accepted as truth that he "couldn't get his
mouth around the essential yes" (BM, 98) and thus each, like
Wright, is "not without honor except in his own country" (BM,
433).

There are several minor figures in the narratives who play a
similar role—men whose careers as truth-sayers result in their
being labeled as cynics or disruptive forces. Mr. Robbins, who
works many years for Moorehouse, is such a character, but Jerry
Burnham, the radical newspaperman who appears in the narratives of Janey, Eveline, and Mary French, is the more developed
figure. Because Robbins and Burnham know the truth but lack the
heroic strength of the biography figures, they sink into moroseness
and drunken self-contempt. Yet they too reveal that some men can
see and speak honestly, as Jerry does about the war, the peace con-
ference, and the communist involvement in the left-wing movement.

Far more significant among the narrative figures similar to the
truth-sayers of the biographies are the major characters who have
the ability to see the truth but who betray their vision because of
their commitment to the big money. Blanche Gelfant has written
perceptively about the failures in identity among the characters of
U.S.A., that "their flatness and helplessly drifting quality is largely
a result of their inability to find inner reality."[13] Several of the major characters in U.S.A., however, do not so much fail to find their
identity as suppress an identity which threatens their success. We

sense in the early lives of Charley Anderson, Dick Savage, and Margo Dowling qualities of character and temperament which are their essential natures. Charley's love of engines, Dick's aesthetic sensibility, and Margo's responsiveness to others have sparks of life in their early careers which, if properly nurtured, might have grown into sustaining identities. But each lacks the courage to sacrifice and fight for what he is, and thus each, despite his ostensible success, lives an artificial and unhappy life. Our last glimpse of Margo is of a doll-like figure created to fulfill a public role. But it is the fates of Charley and Dick which most fully enforce the implicit theme of the truth-sayer biographies that it is better to be martyred or misunderstood than to suppress a truthful vision of oneself for the success that this suppression might bring. The drunken and whoring Anderson, prone to prolonged binges and self-destructive accidents, and the deceitful, treacherous, self-hating Dick Savage are biting studies in the spiritual malaise which a knowledge of self-betrayal can bring. Their narratives are intended to move us not so much to moral condemnation (though there is some of this) as to a sense of the tragic waste of a potential for vision and honesty.

Perhaps the fullest expression of the tragic theme in the narratives is contained in the character and life of Mary French. Mary's career is that of an average but enlightened American. A sensitive and insightful young woman (a key is that she reads and admires Veblen while at college), Mary sees at first hand in the Chicago slums and Pennsylvania mine and mill towns the degradation of working class American life. Her radicalism arises less from a political ideology than from a responsiveness to misery and pain. Yet Mary's ability to help the working class is constantly compromised by her disastrous love affairs with various left-wing leaders, affairs which allegorize the ways in which an aroused social conscience can be weakened and limited in America. Her first relationship is with Gus, an uneducated young Pittsburgh radical with whom she unconsciously falls in love. Then she meets George Barrow and lives with him for some time in Washington while serving as his secretary. In New York she takes in and nurses Ben Compton; they fall in love and live together while he continues his union organizing. And finally she lives with Don Stevens, a newspaperman turned communist leader. Each of the affairs ends poorly. Gus is beaten and sent to jail for his activities; Barrow, Mary realizes, is selling out the labor movement, and she leaves him; Ben decides that a family will handicap his work in the party and drifts away; and Stevens leaves her at party orders in order to marry a foreign comrade. In each instance, Mary's capacity to give of herself is cast aside or betrayed for reasons that constitute the fate of the informed sensibility which seeks to respond to the needs and conditions of most Americans. Her potential for truth-saying is not so much suppressed as prevented from full beneficial expression, and we leave her not guilt-ridden but worn and wasted by her constantly thwarted efforts to fulfill her love for man and mankind.

The most cogent depiction in *U.S.A.* of man's ability to see and act despite the stranglehold of institutions and institutionalized language in America occurs in the career of the authorial persona portrayed in the Camera Eye. With some recent exceptions, this portion of the novel has long been misunderstood. Adopting the position expressed by Dos Passos himself in a late interview,[14] many readers have considered the Camera Eye merely a device to "drain off" the subjective from the creative process and thus somehow ensure the greater objectivity of the remainder of the novel. Or it has been taken to be a device which seeks to demonstrate the ability of the private consciousness to survive in the modern world. Both of these views of the nature and function of the Camera Eye tend to ignore two of its principal qualities. First, the substance of the Camera Eye stream of consciousness is less similar to Molly's reverie at the close of *Ulysses* than to Bloom's thoughts as he wanders during the day. The stream-of-consciousness material is not "pure" interior monologue but consists of the constant intertwining of exterior event and interior reflection, in which the "world outside" plays an important role in the world of consciousness. Second, the consciousness depicted in the Camera Eye is not static. The fifty-one episodes form a kind of novel of development, in which the protagonist, after a number of false starts and difficulties, comes to see his proper role in life and begins to undertake it.[15]

The notion that Dos Passos intended the Camera Eye to dramatize his own intellectual and emotional development is supported by the presence in other portions of the novel of similar reflections of his changing attitudes and values. During the seven or eight years of the genesis and composition of *U.S.A.*, from approximately 1927 to 1935, Dos Passos' commitment to the radical left underwent considerable change. As Daniel Aaron has noted, Dos Passos' radicalism "simmered in the early twenties, boiled furiously between 1927 and 1932 [the period during which he wrote the first two novels of the trilogy], and began to cool thereafter."[16] This shift in Dos Passos' degree of endorsement of the Left can be seen most clearly in his treatment of the radical newspaperman Don Stevens. Throughout the trilogy Stevens and George Barrow frequently appear together in complementary roles. Whether in Washington and New York before the war or Paris during and after it, Barrow is always the soft-centered and self-serving labor leader while Stevens is a sympathetically portrayed radical and, later, enthusiast of the Russian Revolution. When we encounter them in *The Big Money*, however, Barrow is unchanged but Stevens has become a coldly calculating and deceptive party functionary. The depiction of Marxism itself undergoes a similar change. In Mac's narrative in *The 42nd Parallel*—and particularly in the portrayal of Mac's radical printer uncle—Marxism is endorsed as offering an apt description of the nature of class warfare in America. But in his dramatization of the role of Marxism in Ben Compton's life at the close of *Nineteen Nineteen* and throughout *The Big Money*, Dos Passos suggests the baneful personal and social consequences of a programmatic and religiously held economic theory.

Dos Passos also incorporated into his portrayal of several of the biography and narrative figures themes which suggest his absorption in the possibility of growth in vision by someone of his own class. Among the biographies, Jack Reed and Paxton Hibben are depicted as figures who despite "four years under the ethercone" (FP, 301) at Harvard and Princeton awake to an understanding of the world as it is rather than as the conventional lies of their class would have it be. Dick Savage's career as a Harvard aesthete and as an ambulance driver in France and Italy closely parallels Dos Passos' as caught in the Camera Eye. But Dick, though he does develop in insight, lacks the moral courage to fight the system and thus descends into self-hate and spiritual death.

The Camera Eye persona develops despite two related handicaps. He must escape the narrow vision both of his class and of a self-imposed aestheticism if he is to grow in an understanding of the world as it is and thereby assume his proper role in life. His "education" begins as a child when he skates on a pond near the mills. He is warned of the "muckers . . . bohunk and polack kids" and contrasts them with "we clean young American Rover Boys handy with tools Deerslayers played hockey Boy Scouts and cut figure eights in the ice Achilles Ajax Agamemnon" (FP, 81). The imagery here and frequently elsewhere in the Camera Eye portions of the trilogy expresses a condition which the Camera Eye persona finally openly acknowledges in one of his last segments when he cries, "all right we are two nations" (BM, 462). It is an imagery of two classes divided not only by wealth and power but by the language of degradation on the one hand and of mythic prowess and nobility on the other. By the time the Camera Eye persona has reached Harvard, he has begun to awaken to social awareness but feels himself bound by the code of the gentleman aesthete: "don't be a grind be interested in literature but remain a gentleman don't be seen with Jews or Socialists" (FP, 302). His participation in the war, because European conditions vividly reveal the disparity between the strong and the weak and between language and reality, moves him toward involvement as well as insight. His war responses contain a biting edge of anger which presages action, as in the comment that "Up north they were dying in the mud and the trenches but business was good in Bordeaux" (FP, 364), or in the front-line vision of "the grey crooked fingers the thick drip of blood off the canvas the bubbling when the lungcases try to breathe the muddy scraps of flesh you put in the ambulance alive and haul out dead" (NN, 101).

After the war, however, the Camera Eye persona is attracted by the excitement of traveling and by Greenwich Village bohemianism. Not until the late 1920s does the "two nations" theme again move him deeply. At this point he faces a conflict between his newly activated social conscience and his personal doubts about his ability to play a role in the struggle. He is also troubled by the conflict between the high idealism of his thoughts about "the course of history and what leverage might pry the owners loose from power and bring back (I too Walt Whitman) our storybook democracy" (BM, 150) and the pull of more personal desires and needs, as is suggested by the images of "dollars are silky in her hair soft in her dress sprout in the elaborately contrived rosepetals that you kiss become pungent and crunchy in the speakeasy dinner" (BM, 151). So he "peel[s] the speculative onion of doubt" (BM, 151) until the crisis of the Sacco-Vanzetti case persuades him that personal and literary activism must be his course. Standing in Plymouth, where Vanzetti lived and the pilgrims landed, he thinks:

> how can I make them feel how our fathers our uncles haters
> of oppression came to this coast   how say   Don't let them

scare you   how make them feel who are your oppressors
America
    rebuild the ruined words worn slimy in the mouths of
lawyers districtattorneys collegepresidents judges   without
the old words the immigrants haters of oppression brought
to Plymouth how can you know who are your betrayers
America (BM, 437)

To "rebuild the old words," he now realizes, is his function and
commitment—to speak truly and movingly about the misuse of the
great and noble terms—liberty, freedom, democracy—and so to
help recreate their meaning and potency.
    The deaths of Sacco and Vanzetti lead to anger but also to a
hardening of this commitment:

America our nation has been beaten by strangers who have
turned our language inside out who have taken the clean
words our fathers spoke and made them slimy and foul. . . .
    all right we are two nations. . . .
    but do they know that the old words of the immigrants
are being renewed in blood and agony tonight do they know
that the old American speech of the haters of oppression is
new tonight in the mouth of an old woman from Pittsburgh
of a husky boilermaker from Frisco . . . the language of the
beaten nation is not forgotten in our ears tonight (BM,
462–63)

"We stand defeated America," the Camera Eye persona cries out at
the close of this segment, but he himself stands confirmed in his
role. At Harlan County, in the last Camera Eye of the trilogy, he
recounts the betrayal of the miners by owners, government, and
conservative labor and concludes with a statement which an-
nounces both temporary defeat and continuing effort: "we have
only words against" (BM, 525).
    In effect, the Camera Eye persona has brought us to the point
in the late 1920s when he committed himself to write *U.S.A.* He
has accepted the premise that "two nations" exist in America in
part because of the betrayal of the language of freedom and democracy and that he, as a writer, can help restore the "ruined
words" through his art. The Camera Eye in *U.S.A.* is thus not only
a typical nineteenth-century development story in which under-

standing is gained through experience. Like such nineteenth-century poems as Whitman's "Out of the Cradle Endlessly Rocking," it also embodies in its story of growth a preoccupation with the growth of an artist's imaginative power and poetic role, a preoccupation which has fulfilled itself in the work we are reading.

U.S.A. thus combines two nineteenth-century forms—the romantic poem of the development of an imaginative sensibility and the Victorian novel of plot. Dos Passos' pervasive interlacing and cross-stitching of character, event, and place in an extremely long work produce the equivalent of the Victorian novel's effect of the presence of an organic authorial voice, of a voice in this instance which shapes through ironic analogues or clusters a coherent and powerful vision of life. The Camera Eye is not an anomaly within this organic voice but is rather a means toward confirming in the drama of an expanding consciousness the validity of the depiction of experience in the other modes.

Dos Passos' brilliant control of his technique and materials persuades us to accept the tragic view of American life portrayed in *U.S.A.* We are persuaded that America has been false to its traditional ideals, that these ideals are manipulated by the wealthy and powerful in order to maintain their status, but that there remains the possibility of struggle and even of renewal. It is true that at the close of the trilogy the "ruined words" appear to be irrecoverable. The advertising man Dick Savage is playing court to Myra Bingham, one of the heirs to Doc Bingham's patent-medicine empire, and is thereby uniting the false word and the false thing. The party apparatus is in control of the radical Left. And Sacco and Vanzetti are dead and the Harlan miners are crushed. "We stand defeated America" is an apt response to these conditions. Nevertheless, Wesley Everett and Joe Hill were willing to die for truth in the past, and Veblen and Frank Lloyd Wright erected monuments of truth for the future. "We have only words against," but words can be as potent a weapon for truth as for falsehood. Out of the conscious ambivalence of this vision Dos Passos has created the vast tragic structure which is *U.S.A.*

John Steinbeck

The Grapes of Wrath

Steinbeck's most famous novel is enshrouded in a number of myths about its origin and nature. Here is a work which appears to be the epitome of the 1930s proletarian novel in that all its good people speak bad English, which sweetens its animal view of human nature with an anomalous mixture of Christian symbolism and scientific philosophy, and which appeals principally on the level of sentimentality and folk humor. *The Grapes of Wrath*, in short, is naturalism suffering the inevitable consequences of its soft thinking and its blatant catering to popular interests.[1]

The Grapes of Wrath is indeed closely linked to the 1930s. Unlike either *Studs Lonigan* or *U.S.A.*, *The Grapes of Wrath* is set entirely within the 1930s and is concerned with a distinctive condition of the depression. The novel is also a work of the 1930s in the sense that it is a product of Steinbeck's artistic maturation during that decade. His first three novels, all of the late 1920s, are marked by excessive fantasy and turgid allegory. In 1930 Steinbeck married Carol Hemmings, met the marine biologist Ed Ricketts, and began to interest himself in economic and social problems.[2] His wife's deep commitment to his career, Ricketts' philosophical naturalism, and the impingement of contemporary social events on his writing seemed to push Steinbeck not into a denial of his earlier "romantic" strain but toward a hybrid form in which symbol making and ideas have a solid base in contemporary life. In the mid-1930s Steinbeck became absorbed in the plight of the migrant farm workers of the central California valleys. He reported their conditions, talked at great length about their ways in the prairie West and California with the sympathetic manager of a government camp,[3] and thus gained an awareness of the substantive detail which crowds *The Grapes of Wrath*.

The Grapes of Wrath is also a depression novel in its often doctrinaire 1930s economic, social, and political ideas. As late as 1960, in a reminiscence of the 1930s, Steinbeck still held a melodramatic view of the decade, one in which Hoover epitomized the forces of social evil and Roosevelt of good.[4] *The Grapes of Wrath* has something of the same character. Evil is epitomized by the great banks and corporations which oppress the common worker and manipulate, by fear, the lower middle class. The California portion of the novel even enacts an American version of European fascism, in which the deputies and vigilantes are proto-fascists and the migrants are hounded Jews. To this 1930s mix, Steinbeck adds an appropriately Marxist interpretation of history and of economic processes. The migrants can be exploited because labor is abundant, the "lesson of history" is that the increasing chasm between the haves and the have-nots will result in revolution, and organization of the masses—from camp sanitation committees to labor unions—is the solution to all social problems.

There is also an element of truth in the view that *The Grapes of Wrath* contains an uneasy amalgam of what Edmund Wilson called "biological realism"[5] and an overapparent Christian symbolism. Few readers today would accept Wilson's remark of 1940 that Steinbeck's characters are "so rudimentary that they are almost on the animal level" or the obsessive concern in the 1950s and early 1960s with Biblical parallels in the novel.[6] Nevertheless, the Joads are primitive folk who live close to the natural processes of life, Steinbeck does occasionally indulge in a blatant animism (the turtle crossing the road is a famous example), and the Joads' exodus and Casy's life and death are immediately evocative of Christian myth.

Perhaps the most troublesome matter involving the background of *The Grapes of Wrath* in recent decades has been the relationship between the themes of the novel and the philosophical ideas expressed by Steinbeck in his *Sea of Cortez*. Ostensibly a record of a voyage in 1940 by Steinbeck and Ricketts to study marine life in Lower California, *Sea of Cortez* also contains a number of philosophical meditations. The most significant of these is an "Easter Sermon" on the advantages of "non-teleological" or "is" thinking.[7] The non-teleological thinker accepts the fatuousness of man's belief that his will can control events and thus concentrates on understanding experience rather than on judging men. Steinbeck also expresses in *Sea of Cortez* a belief in group identity,[8] an identity which he elsewhere calls the "phalanx." As individuals, all creatures, including man, are usually weak and unknowing; as members of a group they can "key in" to the strength and knowledge of the group. A group can thus have a distinctive identity. As Steinbeck wrote in a letter of 1933, when he first became interested in this idea, "the fascinating thing to me is the way the group has a soul, a drive, an intent, an end, a method, a reaction and a set of tropisms which in no way resembles the same things possessed by the men who make up the group. These groups have always been considered as individuals multiplied. And they are not so. They are beings in themselves, entities."[9]

The two ideas, non-teleological thinking and the phalanx, have long been thought to be the product of Steinbeck's association with Ed Ricketts, but they have also been viewed as irreconcilable ideas both in *Sea of Cortez* and in Steinbeck's fiction. The amoral passivity of "is" thinking and the possibility for beneficial and self-directed group action by the phalanx appear to be incompatible, and "is" thinking in particular seems to be foreign to the moral indignation present in much of Steinbeck's fiction of the decade. But with the recent publication of Richard Astro's *John Steinbeck and Edward F. Ricketts: The Shaping of a Novelist* and Elaine Steinbeck and Robert Wallsten's *Steinbeck: A Life in Letters* it can be seen that the problem in fact does not exist. Although both Steinbeck's and Ricketts' names appear on the title page of *Sea of Cortez*, it was always believed that Steinbeck himself wrote the narrative portion of the book and that he therefore assumed full responsibility for all of the ideas in that portion. We now know, however, that Steinbeck incorporated verbatim sections from Ricketts' unpublished philosophical writing including the passage on non-teleological thinking.[10] Although Steinbeck occasionally used or referred to Ricketts' non-teleological beliefs, he was absorbed most of all during the 1930s, as his letters reveal, by the phalanx idea. He could thus either ignore or contradict "is" thinking when other, more compelling beliefs attracted him. In *Sea of Cortez*, for example, the narrator of the voyage (here presumably Steinbeck) records his anger at the Japanese factory fishing boats which were depleting the waters off Lower California and thus causing hardship among the Mexicans.[11] And so in *The Grapes of Wrath* itself Casy's early defense of non-teleological thinking—"There ain't no sin and there ain't no virtue. There's just stuff people do"[12]—is clearly in the context of an attack on a puritan sexual morality. The issue of the anomaly of Steinbeck's non-teleological philosophy is really a non-issue. The concept was largely Ricketts', and though Steinbeck does occasionally endorse it in special contexts, his own deepest involvement was in the emotionally and morally compelling social activism implied by the phalanx idea.

Thus, there indeed are primitivist, Marxist, Christian, and scientific elements in *The Grapes of Wrath*. But no one of them is the single most dominant element and none is present in a single and obvious way. Rather, they exist in a fabric of complex interrelationship which constitutes both the power and permanence of *The Grapes of Wrath* as a naturalistic tragedy.

The first two portions of *The Grapes of Wrath*—the Joads in Oklahoma and on the road to California—enforce upon us the realization that the more we come to know and admire the humanity of the Joads the more inhumanely they are treated. Steinbeck's success in involving us in this irony derives in part from his ability to place the Joads within two interrelated mythic sources of value: they are primitives and they are folk. Their "natural" ways and feelings touch upon a core belief which in various forms runs through American life from the Enlightenment to the primitivistic faith of such moderns as Faulkner and Hemingway.

The Joads are close to the natural processes and rhythms of life. They are farmers who have always farmed and hunted. They have little education and little association with town or city. Their unit of social life is the family with its "natural" crests of birth, puberty, and marriage at one end of life and aging and death at the other. Indeed, the Joads seem to live in a pre-tribal stage of social evolution, since their principal contacts are with other families rather than with school, church, or state. Spoken and written expression to them is always a barrier; they communicate largely by action and by an instinctive sensitivity to unspoken feelings. We first encounter them not in person but rather in the long series of anecdotes about them which Tom and Casy share at the opening of the novel, anecdotes which establish their shrewdness, openness, and understanding in a context of crudity and occasional bestiality. But even this texture of animality in their lives helps establish their naturalness.

As primitives, the Joads have an "honest" relationship to their land. They farm to live, not for profit, and out of the intrinsic relationship between their work and their existence there emerges the life-sustaining values of industry and pride as well as an instinctive generosity and compassion. They seem at first lawless because of their opposition to those who wish to remove them from their land, but their experiences on the road reveal that regulation and order in their lives arise organically out of their needs and conditions. The different families meeting each night in make-shift camps along Route 66 quickly establish unwritten codes of behavior which maintain order and equity in the camps.

The care with which Steinbeck molds our sense of the primitive strength of the Joads early in the novel is especially revealed in two areas of their experience. The Joads are attuned to solving the problems of their lives without outside aid. They raise and prepare their own food, they make their own clothes, and they create and maintain their own special form of transportation. We thus come to accept that the Joads are latter-day pioneers, that the myth of the self-sustaining pioneer family still lives in them. But the Joads not only solve problems by the exercise of individual skills but also by the maintenance of a group strength and efficiency. Here Steinbeck is at pains to dramatize his phalanx notion of the distinctive identity of the group. So, for example, in the family councils just before departure or soon after Grandpa's death, the family when it meets to solve its problems becomes a powerful and cohesive single body, "an organization of the unconscious. They obeyed impulses which registered only faintly in their thinking minds" (135).

The Joads are folk as well as primitives; that is, we also experience the comic and the ritualized in their naturalness. For example, the three generations of the Joads constitute a gallery of family folk types: earthy and querulous grandparents, eccentric and even occasionally demented uncles and brothers, cocky and sexually vibrant late adolescents, and over-curious and problem-creating children. Above all, the Joads contain the archetypal center of the folk family, the mother as source of love, wisdom, and strength. The Joads as folk salt the novel with the sexuality and excrementality of folk humor and with the ritualized forms of folk life, particularly of courtship and death. Some of the folk attributes and experiences of the Joads have both a Dickensian predictability of repetitive motif and a freakish humor characteristic of Erskine Caldwell's portrayal of poor whites. (The Joads' discovery of the flush toilet is pure Caldwell.) But the folk element in the lives of the Joads, when combined with the central strain of their primitivism, contributes to rather than diminishes our sense of their basic humanity. The earthiness and humor of the Joads as folk permit Steinbeck to avoid the heavy-breathing and lush prim-

itivism of his early fiction—notably of *To a God Unknown*—and en-
courage us to respond to them not only as symbols but as "real"
people.

The Joads as primitive folk appear to be opposed by the life-
denying forces of the mechanical, institutional, and intellectual. In
Oklahoma these forces are allegorized by the banks and corporations which have the law and wealth on their side but which lack
the human attributes of understanding and compassion. The
forces are symbolized above all by the impersonal and mechanical
tractor which destroys the farmers' homes and by the anonymous
car which attempts to run over the turtle as it goes about its "business" of spreading the seed of life. Yet the mechanical and the
commercial are not inherently evil. The Joads' jerry-built truck
soon becomes a symbol of family unity as well as a means of fulfilling their striving for a better life. And the small businessmen along
the road and the small California ranchers are themselves threatened with destruction. If the tractor were owned and used by the
Joads, Steinbeck tells us, it would be a beneficial mechanical force.
The real evils in the Joads' life are thus not the abstractions of the
mechanical or the institutional but the human failings of fear, anger, and selfishness. Those who cheat or beleaguer or harass the
Joads in Oklahoma and on the road and in California may symbolize the opposition of the structured in life to the natural but
they are above all greedy or frightened men who wish to preserve
or add to what they own. Steinbeck's depiction of this essentially
human conflict suggests that his attempt in *The Grapes of Wrath* was
not to dramatize a labored and conventional primitivistic ethic. It
was rather to engage us, within the context of primitivistic values,
in one of the permanent centers of human experience, that of the
difficulty of transcending our own selves and thereby recognizing
the nature and needs of others.

Although the Joads as a family are the matrix of this growth, the
process of transcendence occurs most pointedly and fully in the
lives of Tom, Ma, and Casy, The experiences of these characters
illustrate Steinbeck's faith in the ability of man to move from what
he calls an "I" to a "We" consciousness.[13] The "conversion" of Tom,
Ma, and Casy to a "We" state of mind is both the theme and the
form of *The Grapes of Wrath*; it is also Steinbeck's contribution both
to the naturalistic theme of the humanity of all sorts and conditions of men and to the naturalistic tragic novel of the 1930s.

Tom is initially the symbol of "natural man." He is big and rawboned, is uncomfortable in store-bought clothes, and he can roll a cigarette or skin a rabbit expertly. He has humor, understanding, and a common-sense shrewdness and he is proud and independent. He judges men and events with generosity of spirit, but his faith in his judgment and in a natural order in life has been tempered by his imprisonment for killing a man in self-defense during a drunken brawl. He cannot understand his punishment and emerges from prison with the belief that it is better to live from moment to moment than to seek to understand and thus to plan.

If Tom is natural man, Ma is natural woman in the roles of wife and mother. Steinbeck's initial description of her renders with a blatantly exultant religiosity her character and function as preserver of the family:

> Her full face was not soft; it was controlled, kindly. Her hazel eyes seemed to have experienced all possible tragedy and to have mounted pain and suffering like steps into a high calm and a superhuman understanding. She seemed to know, to accept, to welcome her position, the citadel of the family, the strong place that could not be taken. . . . And from her great and humble position in the family, she had taken dignity and a clean calm beauty. . . . She seemed to know that if she swayed the family shook, and if she ever really deeply wavered or despaired the family would fall, the family will to function would be gone. (100)

Tom's power lies in his pride and shrewdness, Ma's in her capacity to love and in her sense of continuity. To her, life is not a series of beginnings and endings but rather "all one flow, like a stream, little eddies, little waterfalls. . . . Woman looks at it like that. We ain't gonna die out. People is goin' on—changin' a little, maybe, but goin' right on" (577). If Tom represents natural strength, Ma represents natural religion. She is appalled by the religion of fear and sin which she encounters in the woman in black at Grandma's death and in the "Jesus-lover" at Weedpatch. Her religion is of love, and love to her means constant rededication to preserving the family, just as Tom's strength means solving the problems which this pledge demands.

Whereas Tom and Ma are fully realized both as characters and as symbols, Casy functions principally as a symbol. Dissatisfied with conventional religious truth because it runs counter to his own impulses, he seeks to find God in his own spirit rather than in Bible or church. On the morning of the Joads' departure, he is asked to say grace before breakfast. He seizes the opportunity to tell them of his attempt to commune with God in the hills. He felt a oneness with all things, he explains,

> "An' I got thinkin', on'y it wasn't thinkin', it was deeper down than thinkin'. I got thinkin' how we was holy when we was one thing, an' mankin' was holy when it was one thing. An' it on'y got unholy when one mis'able little fella got the bit in his teeth an' run off his own way, kickin' and draggin' an' fightin'. Fella like that bust the holiness. But when they're all workin' together, not one fella for another fella, but one fella kind of harnessed to the whole shebang—that's right, that's holy." (110)

The Joads, however, scarcely listen; they are absorbed in the expectation of breakfast. And Casy does not really understand the implications of his insight into the nature of "holiness" as a kind of phalanx of group oneness. The journey of the Joads, and particularly of Tom, Ma, and Casy, is thus not so much to California as toward a full understanding and acceptance of this vision of human sanctity and strength.

The "I" quality of life, man's selfishness in its various forms, is the dominant force in the Oklahoma portion of *The Grapes of Wrath*. It exists not only in the corporate "I" of the banks and land companies which are displacing the Joads but in the Joads themselves. Their intense and instinctive commitment to family unity and preservation is a superficially attractive but nevertheless narrow and limited form of self-absorption. It has already been revealed as ineffective in that it has not prevented their eviction. And the local young man who is driving the tractor which is bulldozing their home displays its vital flaw when he says, in defense of his turning against his own people, " 'You got no call to worry about anybody's kids but your own' " (51). Not to worry about someone else's children, however, as the novel makes clear in incident after incident involving a child, is to aid not only in the destruction of the children of others but of one's own.

The Oklahoma section of the novel also contains several strains of "We" thinking, strains which emerge more clearly and fully as the novel proceeds. The famous description of the turtle crossing the road is a parable not only of persistence within nature—of the turtle continuing his journey with ingenuity and strength despite hazards and setbacks—but of the relatedness and unity of all life. The turtle unconsciously carries in a crevice of his shell a seed from a plant he has brushed against; he thus has both a specific goal and the general function of contributing to the perpetuation of other forms of life. Tom and Ma at this point are somewhat like the turtle in that while pursuing a specific narrow goal they also reveal in several ways an unconscious acceptance of a "We" ethic. Ma, when she reflects on the number of tenant farmers being evicted, moves instinctively toward a Marxist idea of unity: "'They say there's a hun'erd thousand of us shoved out. If we was all mad the same way . . . —they wouldn't hunt nobody down'" (104). And Tom accepts without question Muley's observation that "'If a fella's got somepin to eat an' another fella's hungry—why, the first fella ain't got no choice'" (66). But these "We" qualities, like those of the turtle and other animals, are both instinctive and ungeneralized. They have not taken on the human qualities of consciousness and abstraction, the qualities which Steinbeck later in the novel associates with "Manself"—the distinctive ability of man to give up something material, even life itself, for a concept. The "We" in man, though an attribute of the universal potential for a phalanx identity, is distinguished by conscious awareness and direction.

The tension between the primitive folk "I-ness" of the Joads' commitment to family and their tentative reaching out toward a "We-ness" continues on the road. Now, however, new conditions and experiences impress on the Joads a greater sense of the meaning and validity of "We." "I-ness" is of course still paramount in their minds, particularly after Grandpa's death raises the specter of eventual dispersal of the family. Their response to the crisis of his death—the decision to bury him by the side of the road—renews a pioneer custom and thus affirms the primacy of the family in the westering experience. But on the road the Joads encounter families like them in intent and need, such as the Wilsons, and so begin to move out of their isolation.[14] And in the wayside camps the Joads begin to realize the benefits of group cooperation. Perhaps most of all they begin to sense the potential strength in the fact that so many share the same condition; they are beginning to shape in their minds the vital difference, as Steinbeck expresses it in an interchapter, between "I lost my land" and "We lost *our* land" (206).

The California experiences of the Joads—and particularly of Ma and Tom—make explicit to them the difference between "I" and "We." This portion of the novel is divided into four segments. The first two (the Hooverville and Weedpatch) demonstrate concretely to the Joads the opposition between the "I" and "We" ways of life; the second two (the peach ranch and the boxcar) demand of them a conscious allegiance either to "I" or "We." The Hooverville and the government camp at Weedpatch represent, as many readers have complained, a loaded contrast in human values. The Hooverville is an allegorical representation of anarchistic animality, of the anger, cruelty, and desperation of men seeking to survive in a world in which they are pitted against each other. Put in Marxist terms, the Hooverville is a free market economy when the supply of labor exceeds demand and when labor is unorganized. The government camp, though it is an island in a hostile sea, is maintained on the principle of the surrender of some individual rights for the greater good of the whole. Its method is organization to achieve group aims, and its operative unit is the committee. Put in Marxist terms, it is the proletarian state.

The Joads are almost immediately involved in the destructive violence of the Hooverville; at Weedpatch they flourish and contribute to the suppression of violence. As throughout the novel, the ethical distinction between the "I" of the Hooverville and the "We" of Weedpatch is revealed by the treatment of children at the two camps. When the Joads arrive at the Hooverville Ma prepares supper and soon finds herself surrounded by starving children. She is torn between her commitment to her own family and her responsiveness to the silently begging children, and can only cry out, "'I dunno what to do. I got to feed the fambly. What'm I gonna do with these here?'" (350). In Weedpatch the problem of hungry children is resolved not by depriving one's own—not by the "I" principle of the conflict between mine and yours—but by maintaining a camp fund which dispenses loans to those in need.

The peach ranch to which the Joads are forced to move in order to get work unites the Hooverville and Weedpatch principles in one volatile setting. Inside the ranch, in a kind of prison, are the families driven to the "I" of scabbing because of their desperate need; outside are striking migrants who have organized to help all migrants. Casy had been separated from the Joads at the Hooverville when he had been arrested for coming to the aid of a man being framed by the deputies. He now reappears as a strike leader and union organizer, and explains his conversion to Tom. "'Here's me, been a-goin' into the wilderness like Jesus to try to find out somepin. Almost got her sometimes, too. But it's in the jailhouse I really got her'" (521). What he had learned in prison, in the incident of the men acting in unison to gain better food, was the principle of group action to achieve just ends. Life had a holy unity both in the wilderness and in jail, but he has discovered in jail that his function was not passively to accept this holiness but to seek actively to render it concrete in social life. Tom, however, doesn't fully understand Casy's explanation, and Casy says, "'Maybe I can't tell you. . . . Maybe you got to find out'" (522).

The vigilantes attack the strikers, and as Casy is about to be clubbed down, he says, "'You fellas don' know what you're doin'. You're helpin' to starve kids'" (527). The first sentence of this speech (and its repetition by Casy just before his death) is often cited as a specific parallel between Casy and Christ. In fact, Casy is a Christ-figure only in the social-activist sense of the Christian life in *The Grapes of Wrath*. The vigilantes are not killing the son of God but children who have been denied their humanity, and Casy is not sacrificed to vouchsafe a heaven for man but to aid man to achieve a better life on earth. Holiness is not a condition between God (or his son) and man but between man and man, between all the members of the "whole shebang," as Casy put it earlier. Helping to starve children is thus unholy or parallel to killing Christ; helping to create a society in which children will be fed is man's true Christ-like role on earth.

Even though Tom fails to grasp Casy's meaning at this point, he has been growing in understanding. True, his two acts of involvement so far—his coming to the aid of the Hooverville migrant earlier and of Casy now—were instinctive responses to blatant acts of bullying. But he has also been absorbing a sense of the social injustice and of the fundamental inhumanity in the condition of the migrants which is now reaching the level of consciousness. He realizes that the landowners wish not only to employ the migrants but to turn them into a kind of obedient domestic animal. "'They're a-workin' away at our spirits,'" he tells the family. "'They're a-tryin' to make us cringe an' crawl like a whipped bitch. They tryin' to break us'" (381).

In defending Casy, Tom has killed a man and therefore has to live in the fields when the family moves on to pick cotton and live in an abandoned boxcar. Musing over Casy's ideas and experiences, he now accepts what he had earlier neither understood nor had even consciously heard. Casy, he recalls,

> "went out in the wilderness to find his own soul, an' he foun' he didn' have no soul that was his'n. Says he foun' he jus' got a little piece of a great big soul. Says a wilderness ain't no good, 'cause his little piece of a soul wasn't no good 'less it was with the rest, an' was whole. Funny how I remember. Didn' think I was even listenin'. But I know now a fella ain't no good alone." (570)

Tom here expresses both Casy's wilderness vision and his later social expansion and application of that vision. The wilderness (contemplation and passivity) is not a true joining of one's soul to that of all men; only in social unity and action can this be achieved. So Tom decides to pursue a true "We-ness"; like Casy, he will now attempt to organize the migrants.

The Joads, and particularly Ma, move in an analogous direction. In the crisis of Rose's delivery during the flood, the Wainwrights, who are as beleaguered as the Joads, come to their aid. When Ma tries to thank Mrs. Wainwright, she replies,

> "No need to thank. Ever'body's in the same wagon. S'pose we was down. You'd a give us a han'."
> "Yes," Ma said, "we would."
> "Or anybody."
> "Or anybody. Use' ta be the fambly was fust. It ain't so now. It's anybody. Worse off we get, the more we got to do." (606)

So Ma, the staunchest defender of the "I" of the family, has come to accept consciously the principle of "We" embodied in the "anybody" of those in need.

The conclusion of the novel, when Rose of Sharon gives her breast to the starving man in the barn, unites in one symbolic act various themes which have been fully dramatized in the conversions of Tom and Ma. Throughout the novel Rose's pregnancy has represented one of the major strands in the primitive character of the Joads as a family. Her child-bearing is honored because it is a contribution to family continuity, and it constitutes, because of her intense self-preoccupation, the inward-turning nature of the family. But with the birth of her still-born child—a child who is the last "starving kid" of the novel—she is freed from these "I" roles. Encouraged by Ma, she can now—in a climactic gesture of conversion—move outward to the "We" of the starving man. She is saying, in effect, that all those who hunger are her children, just as Tom has given himself to the anonymous migrants who require leadership and Ma to the "anybody" who needs.

By the close of the novel the Joads have been stripped clean in several senses. They have lost most of their possessions, including the truck which had served since their departure from Oklahoma as a symbol of family unity. In the family itself, the weak (Grandpa and Grandma) and the irredeemably self-preoccupied (Noah, Connie, and finally Al) have fallen away. Left is a core of Ma and Pa, Uncle John and Rose, and the two children, Ruth and Winfield. With the exception of the children but including Tom, this is a group in which each figure has conformed to the Biblical promise that to lose all is often to gain one's salvation; that is, each has struggled through to a form of "We" consciousness. Tom in his decision to trade a day-to-day existence for militant organizing, Ma in her acceptance at last of commitments beyond that of saving the family, Rose in the translation of her biological self-absorption into an almost blissful giving, Pa in his neglect of his anger at his loss of status in the family as he marshals the boxcar migrants into a group effort to save their dwellings, and even John, in that for once his life-long preoccupation with his guilt is replaced by an outward-directed anger (it is he who sets Rose's dead baby afloat in a box to remind the nearby townspeople that they are starving children)—each has made the journey from "I" to "We."

In one of the major ironic motifs of *The Grapes of Wrath*, this reduction of the Joads to an almost animal struggle for survival also bares fully their essential humanity, their Manself. Throughout the novel the migrants' poverty has been viewed by others as an index of their inhumanity. The gas station attendant at Needles cries, "'Them goddamn Okies got no sense and no feeling. They ain't human. A human being wouldn't live like they do. A human being couldn't stand it to be so dirty and miserable'" (301). But it is the very absence of that which defines humanity to the limited understanding which at last helps shape the penetrating clarity of spiritual insight of the Joads and thus enables them to discover a transcending sense of oneness with all men.

Our understanding of and response to the Joads' journey to awareness are aided by a number of fictional devices. Of these, the natural and Biblical symbolism requires little detailed discussion. The one serves to establish certain similarities between the Joads and natural life, the other between them and man's spiritual character. Together they contribute to Steinbeck's theme of the enriching unity of all life, in which the natural is also the spiritual and the spiritual is also the natural. Less obvious in their function are the interchapters and the cyclic structure of the novel. Both serve as forms of editorial commentary through which the Joads' experience is translated into a statement on the human condition. The interchapters have a number of forms, from generalized narrative and prose poem to dramatic exchange and authorial philosophizing. They also vary in content from social realism to expressionistic exaggeration and in tone from humor and satire to bombast and supplication. But they are bound together, whatever their form, content, or tone, by the underlying authorial emotion of anger. Steinbeck uses the narrative of the Joads to involve us in the tragic pathos of the life of a migrant family, and the interchapters to involve us in the anger we must feel when we understand the inhumanity to man which their lives illustrate. The interchapters not only allegorize the Joads into universal figures of the poor and downtrodden but also engage us, through Steinbeck's devices in these sections, in an intensity of emotion usually foreign to allegory and other forms of abstraction. The interchapters are not extraneous to the novel but rather are central to its ability to move us.

Anger, yet an anger which contains an element of hope, is also an important characteristic of the cyclic form of *The Grapes of Wrath*. The novel begins with the Joads poor and landless in a drought-stricken Oklahoma; it ends with them even poorer and still landless in a flooded California. In Oklahoma, the men are at first silent and puzzled but then become "hard and angry and resistant" as they sit "thinking—figuring" (6–7). In California, the men, in a parallel moment, are at first fearful and then angry (592). Anger is thus a source of both strength and continuity. In

California, moreover, anger has found a focus and therefore a potential resolution. Nature, whether drought or flood, is not to blame for the condition of the migrants, nor is the Oklahoma tractor driver or the California deputy or ranch foreman. To blame is the greed exemplified by the economic system, and against this force, the Joads, who have thought and figured, have begun to find an answer in their willingness (as symbolized by Tom) to mold themselves into a group force equal in strength. So the last two chapters of the novel end with images of renewal in the midst of the carnage. After the starvation of the winter, "Tiny points of grass came through the earth, and in a few days the hills were pale green with the beginning year" (592); and after the Joads are driven from the boxcar by the flood, Rose nurses the starving man in the barn.

Much that is central in *The Grapes of Wrath* as a naturalistic novel of the 1930s can be understood by noting the remarkable number of similarities, as well as some significant differences, between it and an earlier naturalistic novel of social conflict in California, Frank Norris' *The Octopus*. In both works a struggle for land occurs within a cycle of natural growth, and in both the weaker figures in the conflict—the wheat ranchers and the migrants—suffer a tragic defeat. But in both instances, the most insightful and feeling of those crushed—Annixter, Vanamee, and Presley, and Tom, Ma, and Casy—struggle through to an understanding both of the underlying nature of the conflict and the essential nature of life. The three young men in *The Octopus* learn that the machinations of men cannot affect the omnipotence and benevolence of the natural process of growth, and the Joads learn to accept the oneness of all existence. Both works are fundamentally naturalistic despite these religious overtones. As is also true of *The Octopus*, the naturalism of *The Grapes of Wrath* resides in the theme that man can find in verifiable natural and social life the basic truths he should live by. In *The Octopus* the continuity of life is discovered not in the Pauline symbol of the seed—that man shall be reborn in heaven—but in the real seed, that man and nature reproduce themselves. And in *The Grapes of Wrath*, Casy's discovery that all things are united in holiness is only a vaguely felt concept until its meaning is completed by his finding that oneness is union organization and that holiness is the power to correct injustice. Men may come to know these truths initially by an instinctive or intuitive reaching out, but the truth itself must be not only felt but also observed and validated in experience. Both novels are thus conversion allegories, but the "religion" to which the characters are converted is that of the sanctity of life itself rather than of some aspect of man, God, or nature which is different from or superior to the life we lead and know.

The Grapes of Wrath also has its own distinctive character as a naturalistic novel of the 1930s. *The Octopus* proclaims that "all things, surely, inevitably, resistlessly work together for good,"[15] since the natural process of growth is both omnipotent and beneficent. Although the railroad monopoly is a bad thing which affects individuals adversely, it does not adversely affect mankind in general, since society and its conflicts are subsumed under the cosmic beneficence of the natural order. Men have died in the struggle for a crop of wheat, but the wheat itself will feed the starving millions of India. Steinbeck's perspective is quite different. Much of the fruit grown by the San Joaquin ranchers doesn't reach anyone because it is destroyed to maintain high prices, an act which aids the wealthy but harms the poor, including the migrant children who hunger for the oranges they see all around them. Steinbeck views the American economic system not as part of a natural process but as a baneful social illustration of the "I" principle. Men can and must struggle through to a "We" activism of camp committees and unions rather than accept that good will eventually accrue to the greatest number through cosmic beneficence. Although Steinbeck in *The Grapes of Wrath* occasionally appears to be endorsing a Marxist theory of historical necessity by his references to the inevitability of class conflict if class divisions continue to grow, he is really endorsing a naturalistic version of a traditional social gospel activism in which one's beliefs must be realized in social life as well as be expressed in the temple.

Some of the obvious and often noted defects of *The Grapes of Wrath* stem from its character as a 1930s naturalistic novel, though a good many of these are less disturbing if the allegorical mode of the novel is at once accepted. Parables such as the turtle crossing the road, characters who exist principally as symbols, the hell-paradise contrast of the Hooverville and Weedpatch—these are major weaknesses only if one adopts the notion that naturalism is limited to the probabilities of social realism. Much more significant as a flaw in *The Grapes of Wrath* is the conflict between its tragic and social impulses. Steinbeck asks us to respond to the fate of the Joads with the compassion we bring to other accounts of men who must be stripped naked and suffer before they can understand the needs of the poor naked wretches around them. But he also generates intense anger toward those causing the misery of the Joads and points out ways in which their condition can be improved. The two intents seem to be related. It is the economic system as a whole which is the equivalent of the Joads' initial "I" values. Thus, compassion for their suffering as they move toward a "We" consciousness, and anger at the economic system for failing to undergo this change appear to be coordinate sentiments. But in fact the presence of these two emotions both diffuses and confuses the tragic theme and form of the novel. Steinbeck has succeeded so well in engaging us in the nature and quality of the Joads as primitive folk that the family assumes a validity at odds with his ultimate goal for them. We wish the Joads to find a better life in California, but we are not really persuaded that the committees and unions and other activities which represent the "We" principle in their lives are really better than the folk inwardness and the clearly definable entity that is their family. Here we are perhaps victims of a change in perspective since the 1930s in that we are no longer convinced that committees are inherently superior to other forms of awareness and action. We are also reacting in a way unforeseen by Steinbeck to his conviction that the humblest man can rise to the wisest thoughts. Steinbeck believed that it would be primarily the "thoughts"—the acceptance by the Joads of "We-ness"—which would hold us. But instead it is the Joads themselves who are the source of the enduring power of the novel.

The Late 1940s and Early 1950s

Preface

In a series of influential essays written during the early and mid-1940s, a number of major critics announced the death of American naturalism. Philip Rahv noted its "utter debility,"[1] while Lionel Trilling and Malcolm Cowley located its fatal weakness in its metaphysical and fictional simplicity.[2] One reason for this assault, as Willard Thorp pointed out, was that the literary gods of the period were Kafka, Dostoevsky, and James, writers whose complex themes and symbolic forms appeared to be the antithesis of naturalism.[3] Another and less frequently acknowledged reason was political in origin. American naturalism of the 1890s was largely apolitical, but in the 1930s the movement was aligned with the left in American politics and often specifically with the Communist Party. In the revulsion against the party which swept the literary community following the Soviet purges of the late 1930s and the Russian-German pact of 1939, it was inevitable that naturalistic fiction would be found wanting because the naturalists of that decade, it was now seen, had so naively embraced some form of communist belief. The critics who most vigorously attacked the naturalism of the 1930s in the decades which followed were usually those—like Rahv, Trilling, and Cowley—who themselves had held radical beliefs in the 1930s. What better way to cleanse their own ideological consciences, as well as to purge America of an infatuation with an alien and destructive political ideal, than to attack the fallen god of naturalism.

Yet at this very moment of critical rejection of naturalism and of the complementary New Criticism enthusiasm for lyric forms and orthodox belief, American literary naturalism, in the form of the early novels of Norman Mailer, William Styron, and Saul Bellow, once more came upon the scene. From the perspective of our own time, we can see that these and other new writers felt more continuity between their own literary ideals and those of the naturalists of the 1930s than did the critics of their day. Mailer, Styron, and Bellow were too young in the early 1930s to be "tainted" by communism, but they were not too young, by the late 1930s and early

1940s, to be responsive to the work of Farrell, Dos Passos, and Steinbeck.[4] Mailer later acknowledged the powerful impact upon him of *Studs Lonigan*, *U.S.A.*, and *The Grapes of Wrath* when he discovered them as a college freshman,[5] and both Mailer and Bellow viewed their early work as in the tradition of social realism pioneered by Dreiser.[6] Styron, of course, responded most of all to Faulkner, but the Faulkner of the 1930s can be plausibly viewed as a Southern exponent of several major naturalistic qualities in the fiction of the decade.

These new writers of the late 1940s and early 1950s identified with a 1930s frame of mind because they felt that their own age was also threatened by a loss of freedom. But now the sense of a tragic failure in American life was not triggered by the "mere" collapse of the economic system. The extermination camps, the atom bomb, the cold war in Europe and hot war in Korea, the McCarthy witch hunts—all contributed to a sense of malaise, of individual values and freedoms under immense pressure, which appeared similar to but far greater than the pressure of the depression on traditional beliefs about the nature and destiny of the individual in America. The American economic system contributed to the tragic fates of Studs, Charley Anderson, and the Joads, but one of the impulses behind the depiction of their lives was the conviction that corrupt and destructive systems could be changed—that men of greater awareness and strength (a Danny O'Neill, a Thorstein Veblen, or a converted Tom Joad) could work for a better life for themselves and for others. But these events of the war years and post-war period offered massive evidence of the impotence of the informed will when confronted by the atavistic destructiveness of human nature and the vast, uncontrollable power of the social and political institutions of modern life. The distinctive note of the age was not the hope implicit in tragedy but the chaos present in the struggle for survival and power.

It has been conventional to identify the absorption by the writers of the time in the beleaguered individual attempting to survive in a world devoid of traditional meaning with the impact of French existentialism in America. By the late 1940s Sartre and Camus were being widely read and discussed in America, and there is little doubt that young writers of the period were as alive to their ideas as the young writers of the 1930s had been to Marxism. But in fact, as the best critics of the relationship between existentialism and American post-war writing have noted, the resemblances between the two movements are principally the result of an "affinity of mind" and a "shared consciousness" and are thus best studied as "mutually illuminating" rather than as the effect of the influence of one literature upon another.[7] French existentialism had its roots in the appeal to the contemporary French mind of specific late nineteenth-century philosophical ideas as aids in the explanation of twentieth-century European life. American thought of the late 1940s and early 1950s had an analogous nature and origin. The felt sense of many American intellectuals of the post-war period that communal life and belief were chaotic and irrational and that the only valid source of value lay in individual experience echoed both American naturalism of the 1890s and contemporary French existentialism. For these post-war American writers, the supernatural support of ethical systems was not only unproven but patently untrue; there remained only the individual seeking meaning in his own immediate experience. Thus there occurs a retreat both in existentialism and in the American naturalistic novel of the late 1940s and early 1950s from systems, codes, and structures in any form—from the army and its hierarchy of power, from the family, and from the "adoptive" mechanisms of society. And thus there is the centering of an oblique value on the seeker of the unknown in himself and life.

The deep roots in American life of the romantic individualism underlying this belief are readily apparent. What distinguishes this belief from that of an Emerson and therefore turns it in the direction of naturalism are both its tragic cast and its social emphasis. Defeat is now the natural condition of man, and defeat often means either the failure of life to answer the questions put to it or the answer by life with the resounding "Nothing" which Milton and Helen Loftis believe they hear. But those who nevertheless continue to seek answers in the face of evident defeat do so, as Henry Fleming and Carrie did and as Augie March does now, not in the context of nature or of the "natural" in man but in interaction with their fellow men and often in the city or the group. Meaning must be discovered, if it can be discovered, for oneself and is thus often solipsistically destructive, but it nevertheless is a meaning which has its origin in the collision between self and a particularized social reality.

The naturalistic novel of the late 1940s and early 1950s thus has its origin in traditional themes of the naturalistic novel which are lent even greater authority and resonance by their resemblance to themes in the principal intellectual movement of the post-war period. *The Naked and the Dead, Lie Down in Darkness,* and *The Adventures of Augie March* are in part "debate" novels. Each in its own way undertakes to represent the opposing claims made upon the individual by the determining factors in his experience and by his quests for a distinctive meaning for himself and for a distinctive fate. Each novel fails to resolve this conflict or debate except for the depiction of the tragic fate of most men who seek. The conflict is discussed openly by the characters or by the narrative voice in *Lie Down in Darkness* and *Augie March* and is expressed allegorically in *The Naked and the Dead.* But whatever the mode of expression the three novels share the naturalistic emphasis on identifying the forces that make for restriction of freedom while not rejecting the search for alternative values. Freedom in this debate is not categorically denied but is rather submitted to a close scrutiny of its nature and efficacy in a world consisting largely of conditions which limit and qualify it.

The form of the naturalistic novel of this period also has its own distinctive emphasis while maintaining the naturalistic commitment to the full portrayal of contemporary life. In the 1930s naturalists sought to invent forms which would help express beliefs about man in relation to specific kinds of social experience and value; thus the panoramic or collectivistic characteristics of the naturalism of that period. In the late 1940s and early 1950s writers pushed this experimental tendency in naturalism in the direction of forms which would represent their interest in fundamental philosophical questions about the nature and condition of man. The social base of naturalistic fiction is still apparent—we are accompanying a platoon on a specific mission or are in a middle class suburb or a Chicago neighborhood—but this material often takes on a non-representational character as the author's interest in ideas impels him toward surreal and expressionistic symbolism. Cummings and the artillery piece and Croft and the mountain, or Peyton Loftis' bird and clock symbolism, or Thea and her eagle— all move naturalism toward Kafkaesque and Dostoevskean modes of expression, modes which most critics of the day failed to recognize because of the naturalistic context in which they occurred.

Naturalistic fiction of the late 1940s and early 1950s has led a precarious and ambivalent existence in recent literary history. When clearly apparent as naturalism because of its sensationalism and because of its author's public statements, as in the instance of

The Naked and the Dead, it is denigrated for this quality. When its naturalism is obscured by more obvious characteristics, such as the Southern gothicism of *Lie Down in Darkness* or the picaresque form of *Augie March*, it is praised for these qualities. But these novels can best be viewed as the third major expression of the American attempt to explore at moments of national stress through highly structured dramatizations of particular social moments the problem of man's belief in his freedom in an increasingly restrictive world.

Norman Mailer

The Naked and the Dead

Much criticism of *The Naked and the Dead* has revolved around the question of the chronological siting of the novel within Mailer's career. As a first novel written shortly after the war, does it look back to the proletarian attitudes and fictional forms of the 1930s? Or does it look forward to the existential activism which Mailer was to endorse in the late 1950s? Despite this difference in historical perspective, the two views share a belief that the novel is seriously flawed. Lacking a firm position in its own moment in time, *The Naked and the Dead* is either a clichéd representation of shopworn 1930s ideas or a fuzzy and ambiguous anticipation of themes which were to emerge more clearly later in Mailer's career.[1]

The Naked and the Dead is in a number of ways a 1930s novel. Mailer himself noted the influence on him of the fiction of that decade when he recalled his discovery of the major works of the 1930s during the winter of 1939/40. "In those sixty days," he noted, "I read and reread *Studs Lonigan, U.S.A.*, and *The Grapes of Wrath*."[2] If this absorption does not itself support Malcolm Cowley's remark that *The Naked and the Dead* could be called "The Studs Lonigan Boys in the South Pacific,"[3] it does suggest that Mailer might have viewed the war as literary object through eyes conditioned by the vision of writers of the previous generation. Thus, in *The Naked and the Dead* the army is a microcosm of the class struggle within American society as a whole. Its officer class is almost universally self-serving, bullying, and hypocritical, while its enlisted men are the crushed masses. In Major Conn, a pig-headed, ignorant, and prejudiced professional soldier, Mailer achieves a caricature similar to Art Young's *Masses* cartoons in which a bloated capitalist casually tramples a working man. Mailer's reaction both to the perpetuation of the class struggle in the army and to late 1940s Cold War hysteria helped structure a powerful anti-utopian theme in *The Naked and the Dead* based on 1930s premises. The army, Cummings tells Hearn, is "a preview of the future,"[4] a future in which anti-communism will be "the eventual line to power in America" (427). As an allegorical representation of the future, *The Naked and the Dead* poses an America in which the fascistic General Cummings (his Catholic leanings and latent homosexuality, his ruthless love of power, and his willingness to view men as machines or animals constitute a 1930s vision of the fascist psyche) and the benighted and deeply frustrated Gallegher will rely on anti-communism to suppress such ineffectual liberals as Lieutenant Hearn and Red Valsen. "That really formed the book," Mailer told an interviewer in 1948—"the feeling that people in our government were leading us into war again. The last half was written on this nerve right in the pit of my stomach."[5]

Other characteristic 1930s themes also appear in the novel. The I and R platoon led by Sergeant Croft is an exercise in 1930s social determinism. The Time Machine sections which depict the early life of various members of the platoon demonstrate that men are imprisoned by the conditions and values of the world in which they were bred. And the war itself is portrayed with the literalness of that aspect of 1930s naturalism which assumes that man's bodily functions and physical vulnerability are apt metaphors of the human condition. (At least five characters suffer from diarrhea in the course of the novel. And Hemingway's famous remark that dead soldiers are like carcasses in a slaughter yard is rendered literally by the long scene in which the men of the platoon wander among unburied Japanese corpses. "There damn sure ain't anything special about a man if he can smell as bad as he does when he's dead" (217), someone comments at this point.) And, finally, the outcome of the campaign—Cummings' hollow victory, Hearn's death, and the platoon returning to the treadmill of army life—constitutes an indictment of the emptiness of American life characteristic of 1930s fiction.

The belief that *The Naked and the Dead* can best be seen as an unsatisfactory anticipation of Mailer's later existentialism has its origin in Mailer's famous 1957 essay "The White Negro" and in much of his writing and life-style since the late 1950s.[6] It also owes much to Norman Podhoretz's well-known essay of 1959, "The Embattled Vision of Norman Mailer."[7] In "The White Negro," Mailer expressed his philosophy of existential hip, a philosophy which Podhoretz realized might help explain a number of ambiguities in *The Naked and the Dead*. Mailer, Podhoretz argued, was in *The Naked and the Dead* overtly committed to an anti-war theme in which Croft and Cummings represented a destructive code of power and violence while Hearn and Valsen were figures of liberal sympathies and understanding. But in fact our sense of Mailer's unconscious admiration for Croft and of his contempt for Hearn and Valsen stems from his approval of men who seek to identify their deepest natures by reacting violently against the barriers of life. Thus, *The Naked and the Dead* is not the war in the Pacific seen through the eyes of a 1930s proletarian novelist but the human condition in all its absurdity as viewed by a 1950s existentialist. Mailer seemed to endorse this now widely held belief when he told an interviewer in 1962 that though *The Naked and the Dead* ostensibly depicted the futility of war and violence, beneath these themes was "an obsession with violence. The characters for whom I had the most secret admiration, like Croft, were violent people."[8]

These two approaches to the novel are useful because they suggest Mailer's origins and later direction. They tend, however, to blur the distinctive and integral quality of *The Naked and the Dead* as a powerful novel in its own right. Above all they tend to ignore the quality of *The Naked and the Dead* that I would like to stress— that it is a work in which Mailer has successfully created a symbolic form to express the naturalistic theme of the hidden recesses of value in man's nature despite his tragic fate in a closely conditioned and controlled world.

The Naked and the Dead is perhaps the most successful example in American literary naturalism of a novel which rests an elaborate symbolic and allegorical structure on a base of detailed reportage. Mailer's own interpretation of the form of *The Naked and the Dead* has characteristically been to work against the grain of current opinion. The novel was initially greeted as a triumph of realism, and so Mailer was quick to point out, in a 1948 interview, that it was not "a documentary—a piece of realism" but rather a "highly symbolic book," and that "the number of events that happen to this one platoon couldn't possibly have happened to any one Army platoon in the war."[9] By 1951, however, when Mailer spelled out a conscious Melville influence on the novel, he went on to say, "Of course, I also think that the book will stand or fall as a realistic novel."[10]

As an allegory, *The Naked and the Dead* has some of the characteristics of an inverted fairy tale. The ruler of a remote kingdom (Cummings on Anopopei) faces a challenge to his power (ostensibly the Japanese, but more significantly the resistance to his will offered by his own troops and by Hearn). He sends a young knight on a quest in an effort to overcome the enemy (Hearn and the patrol), but in the end he succeeds more by magic (the accidental and unexpectedly easy victory over the Japanese) than by his skill or by the efforts of the quest. Mailer drew upon a number of other fictional constructs to lend interior shape to this broad overarching allegorical structure. *U.S.A.* offered an example of the symbolic rendering of a society as a whole by the depiction of a gathering of archetypal characters,[11] while *The Grapes of Wrath* was a powerful illustration of the traditional use of the journey as a device to crystallize values and determine fates. *The Red Badge of Courage* and Hemingway's war fiction suggested the symbolic potential of combat as a context for individual self-discovery. More specifically, the floundering and bewilderment of the platoon in *The Naked and the Dead* at most of its tasks suggest Henry Fleming's company, and Hearn's moment of triumphant insight and courage followed quickly by his treacherously arranged death bears a striking resemblance to the fate of Macomber in Hemingway's "The Short Happy Life of Francis Macomber."

The basic nature and shape of *The Naked and the Dead*, however, were most affected by the work of Herman Melville and Theodore Dreiser—Melville directly through *Moby Dick*, Dreiser more obliquely through his fiction as a whole. In an important 1951 interview Mailer commented on "that terrible word 'naturalism.' It was my literary heritage—the things I learned from Dos Passos and Farrell. I took naturally to it, that's the way one wrote a book." Nevertheless, he went on to say, "I was really off on a mystic kick. Actually—a funny thing—the biggest influence on *Naked* was *Moby Dick*. . . . I was sure everyone would know. I had Ahab in it, and I suppose the mountain was Moby Dick."[12]

A parallel statement by Mailer which bears on the conjunction in *The Naked and the Dead* of two seemingly opposing strains of influence occurs in an essay on contemporary American writing which he published in 1963. In the course of his discussion he noted the common distinction between Tolstoy and Dostoevsky—that they "divided the central terrain of the modern novel between them." Tolstoy's concern was with "men-in-the-world," while Dostoevsky's preoccupation was the "terror" of men "exploring the mystery of themselves." He went on to offer *Moby Dick* as "a perfect example of a novel in the second category" and *An American Tragedy* as "a virile example" of the first. Yet some great writers, he continued, straddle both forms (Mailer cited James) and some draw on both while leaning heavily in one direction or the other (Proust and Joyce). Mailer concluded: "The serious novel begins from a fixed philosophical point—the desire to discover reality— and it goes to search for that reality in society, or else must embark on a trip up the upper Amazon of the inner eye."[13] Mailer's fiction after *The Naked and the Dead* can perhaps best be seen as increasingly committed to "the inner eye." But in *The Naked and the Dead* he sought to "straddle both categories"—to write a novel in which he dealt fully and explicitly with the Dreiserian theme of "the mechanics of society"[14] (or, more precisely for Mailer, the nature of power in society) as well as with the Melvillean theme of man's desire to know himself deeply and completely. Mailer offers several additional hints that he attempted in *The Naked and the Dead* to fulfill both aims. In 1948 he commented that the theme of the novel was "the conflict between the beast and the seer in man,"[15] and he explained elsewhere that the titles of both the novel as a whole and the portion devoted to the patrol ("Plant and Phantom") referred to "the conflict between the animal roots of man and his sense of vision," in which the naked are those "obsessed with vision."[16] Man, in short, was a dualistic creature, and a novel could "straddle" this duality in its effort to dramatize both his inner self and the atavistic sources of his social experience. It is out of this venture in straddling that *The Naked and the Dead* assumes its distinctive shape as well as its power and permanence.

The symmetrical balance of the four parts of *The Naked and the Dead* suggests the presence of other symmetrical relationships in the novel. The brief frame sections, "Wave" and "Wake," deal with the beginning and end of the Anopopei campaign. "Argil and Mold" is devoted to the campaign on the north side of the island up to the departure of the patrol, and "Plant and Phantom" is confined almost entirely to the activities of the patrol on the south side. Each of the two central sections contains a carefully balanced series of character relationships. In "Argil and Mold," General Cummings and Lieutenant Hearn discuss the nature of power in a series of meetings, while in an almost independent narrative Sergeant Croft confirms his dominance over the platoon. In "Plant and Phantom," Croft and Hearn and later Croft and Red Valsen vie for control of the platoon. But though Croft and Cummings never meet, and though Hearn has only a few exchanges with Red, it is the similarities in these pairs of characters which supply the underlying symmetry to the novel. Mailer's impulse in establishing likenesses in an upper middle class general and a Texas plains sergeant, in a Harvard graduate and a Montana miner's son, and (toward the end of the novel, with Goldstein and Ridges) in a Brooklyn Jew and an Arkansas farmer, was not to achieve Dickensian paradox but a Dos Passos kind of social allegory. He wished to suggest that a few basic currents run through American life despite our great variety in origin and status.

Mailer's titles for the two central sections of *The Naked and the Dead* reveal his preoccupations in the novel. "Argil" and "mold" are potter's terms; the potter molds argil or clay into the forms he wishes. "Plant" and "phantom" occur early in Nietzsche's *Thus Spake Zarathustra*, when Zarathustra seeks to persuade man that he can rise above conventional notions of himself and reach toward the transcendent self-knowledge of the superman.[17] The major themes of *The Naked and the Dead* are therefore the nature of power and the nature of the self in relation to power, with the first theme dominating "Argil and Mold" and the second "Plant and Phantom."

The theme of man's obsession with power in *The Naked and the Dead* centers on Cummings and Croft. Both men are driven to the pursuit of power by personal and sexual failures early in their lives, and both later compensate for these failures by achieving sexual gratification in the exercise of control over things and men. Because power is a goal in itself, both figures view men as objects to be manipulated—as animals and machines are—for the maintenance of power, and both realize that manipulation or control requires the cultivation in men of fear and hate for those in power. Both find, however, that their desire for absolute and permanent power is thwarted, despite their brilliance and strength, by chance and by group inertia, and both are thus led to offer sacrificial scapegoats for their failure. The striking similarities in Mailer's dramatization of the power drive in two otherwise dissimilar characters suggest that he held a schematized conception of its operation resembling that of a model-theory sociologist.

Perhaps the weakest because the most simplistic element in

Mailer's conception of the drive for power is his rooting of it in the frustrations of early life. Cummings, a boy with an interest in art and a deep love for his mother, is made ashamed of these feelings and thus over-compensates for them by a military career founded on repression of emotion and control over men. And "Croft the Hunter," by instinct an explorer and predator, is fenced in by poverty and by the absence of land and so turns to hate and violence as compensatory expressions of self. The two figures have major sexual crises in early manhood because they view sex as control, as a struggle for power.[18] " 'You're just a goddamn fuggin machine,' " Croft's wife tells him (161), and Cummings finds that in sex with his wife he "must subdue her, absorb her, rip her apart and consume her" (415). When this form of sex fails, the exercise of power in other areas of experience becomes sexual in nature. Croft's yearning for the strength symbolized by the mountain has a sexual coloration, and his response to killing is always sexual. When he and several other members of the platoon surprise a Japanese patrol and kill all but one, Croft "was bothered by an intense sense of incompletion. He was still expecting the burst that Red's gun had never fired. Even more than Red, he had been anticipating the quick lurching spasms of the body when the bullets would crash into it, and now he felt an intense dissatisfaction" (193). For Cummings, the exercise of power has a homosexual cast appropriate to his Oedipal background. Hearn senses the homosexual element in Cummings' wish to dominate him, while the firing of the howitzer later in the novel has for Cummings an effect of phallic control and release, one in which "all his senses felt gratified, exhausted" (566).

Mailer does not believe that all men either desire power or are capable of achieving it, despite Cummings' statement to Hearn that " 'Man's deepest urge is omnipotence' " (323).[19] Major Dalleson, Sergeant Brown, and Corporal Stanley are all appalled by the responsibilities of command; they lack both the will and the native shrewdness to seek power. But in Croft and Cummings the necessary mixture does jell. They have in their make-ups a paradoxical yet potent combination of machine-like efficiency and animal rage. Cummings' strength, Hearn soon realizes, lies in his "almost unique ability to extend his thoughts into immediate and effective action" and thus to make himself "an instrument of [his] own policy" (77, 82). Yet the thwarting of his will stimulates in him "an intense and primitive rage" (106). Croft, during the Japanese offensive, repels an attack on the platoon's river position with steady bursts from a machine gun. Mailer's description of him as welded to the gun in purpose and anger—that Croft "could not have said at that moment where his hands ended and the machine gun began" (152)—captures in one image this paradox.

To maintain power requires a willingness to think of men as "clay" to be molded into the shape one desires by whatever means is necessary to achieve that end. Cummings images Hearn and the American army on Anopopei in precisely this way, as does Croft the platoon.[20] The assumption underlying this view, Hearn comes to realize, is that man is an animal to be tamed. To Cummings, Hearn senses, "He had been the pet, the dog, to the master, coddled and curried, thrown sweetmeats until he had the presumption to bite the master once. And since then he had been tormented with the particular absorbed sadism that most men could generate only toward an animal" (313). Cummings himself thinks of his troops, in a parallel image of absolute control, as machines. In a battle, he muses, "men are closer to machines than humans. . . . Battle is an organization of thousands of man-machines who dart with governing habits across a field, sweat like a radiator, shiver and become stiff like a piece of metal in the rain" (569). Croft, in his disregard for the humanity of his men (a quality communicated symbolically by his crushing of the bird Roth has found and nestled), unconsciously translates into action the philosophical inhumanity of Cummings. The two figures are thus similar both in their own basic inhumanity and in their denial of humanity in their men. Responding to their quest for power with a machine-like and animal strength, they also view all other men as machines and animals. In the conflict between the "beast" and "seer" which Mailer believed to be at the heart of *The Naked and the Dead*, they represent a primitive desire for control which constitutes the "beast" in man.

The skilled pursuer of power realizes that its operative emotions are fear, hate, and contempt. The army is a "fear ladder," Cummings tells Hearn, in which "you're frightened of the man above you and contemptuous of your subordinates" (176). In order to convince Hearn of the truth of this observation, Cummings puts him through a crash course of instruction in the nature of the fear ladder. Forced by Cummings to command recalcitrant enlisted men in meaningless tasks, and forced to humiliate himself before Cummings in the incident of the crushed cigarette, Hearn eventually despises his Headquarters Company subordinates and feels a "clutch of fear and hatred" whenever he sees Cummings (392). Croft is hated by the platoon, yet the men are more comfortable in their complete subservience to him than they are to the proffered comradeship of Hearn. They sense instinctively that Croft's ability to create fear and hate authenticates his power. Red, who has more insight into the workings of the army than the other enlisted men in the platoon, comments ruefully on army medical treatment and by extension on the army as a whole: "Sure, they got it all figured out, Red thought. If they get ya to hate 'em enough you'll crack a nut before you'll go to them, and that way they keep ya on the line. . . . You'd think we weren't men. But immediately afterward he knew that his anger also stemmed from fear" (371).

Those who challenge power—who reject both the omnipotence of those in command and the "fear ladder" of the power structure and who thus assert their humanity—run the risk of being sacrificed as scapegoats by those in control. In an obvious allusion to European history of the previous generation, the scapegoats in *The Naked and the Dead* are a liberal intellectual and a Jew. Hearn is twice sacrificed—first by Cummings, who arranges for him to go on a dangerous patrol because Hearn has challenged his mastery and because Cummings sees in that challenge "a symbol of the independence of his troops, their resistance to him" (318); and then by Croft, who arranges for Hearn's death because he and Hearn are rivals for command of the platoon and because Hearn resists climbing the mountain. In the platoon itself Roth is the sacrificial victim. Weak, inept, an outsider and a complainer, he is always the laggard and on the mountain impedes the climb because of his exhaustion. But Roth is at last driven too far, and in an instinctive bulldog reaction conquers his fear and "knew suddenly that he could face Croft" (665). His death, when he fails to jump a crevasse, follows almost immediately. Like Hearn, he dies because he has resisted power; more specifically, both he and Hearn die because they have resisted the testing of personal power which the climbing of the mountain means to Croft.

Power is not only animal in its origin and nature but also stimulates irrational forces in life which establish its limits and cause its occasional collapse. Those who struggle consciously against power fail, as do Hearn and Red Valsen, because they lack sufficient strength or cleverness or courage. But nevertheless there are several deep currents in life which check the exercise of absolute power. This theme resembles Dreiser's explanation of Frank Cow-

perwood's defeat in *The Titan*. Cowperwood sweeps all before him
in his rise to great power but is eventually thwarted by a natural
force which Dreiser calls the "equation inevitable," a force which in
The Titan takes the form of an instinctive resistance to oppression
by the mass of men when oppression becomes too great. (Similar
dramatizations of a natural opposition to absolute social power occur in Frank Norris's depiction of the wheat in *The Octopus* and in
Steinbeck's account of the migrants as a phalanx in *The Grapes of
Wrath*.) In *The Naked and the Dead*, it is the force of inertia which
slows and often defeats the exercise of complete control over men
and events. Cummings describes the expression of "all human
powers" as an asymmetrical parabola with a "tragic curve" similar
to the trajectory of a shell (570). Rapid movement and a steady
climb are followed by a precipitous fall as air resistance finally
slows and then ends movement. Cummings views "the mass inertia
or the inertia of the masses" (571) as analogous to air resistance,
since his own thrust toward a quick completion of the campaign
has met the resistance of his own troops: "For five weeks the troops
had functioned like an extension of his own body. And now, apparently without cause, . . . he had lost his sensitive control. No
matter how he molded them now the men always collapsed into a
sodden resistant mass like dishrags" (300). Cummings has thus
found that though he can mold individual men—Hearn, for example—he cannot "mold the curve" (571). Another natural condition limiting power is chance. Cummings' brilliant efforts have
little effect on the outcome of the campaign. While Cummings is
away seeking aid from the navy, Major Dalleson accidentally stum-
bles into battle and wins the campaign with "a random play of vulgar good luck" (716). And finally there is the natural limitation of
human intelligence—that despite the obvious superiority of their
minds, men of power are still men rather than supermen. So Cummings, for example, fails to move strongly against the Japanese
because he has misjudged their strength.

All of these natural limits to power appear in the climactic event
of the patrol—the headlong flight of the platoon down the mountain after Croft has kicked a hornet's nest. Croft's desire to express
and test his power by climbing the mountain is thwarted by the
accidental kicking of the nest, by the instinctive recognition of the
platoon while fleeing that the loss of their equipment will preclude
a further attempt on the mountain (a form of mass inertia), and by
Croft's misjudgment of the exhaustion of the men. Matthew Ar-

nold once wrote that life contains "the not ourselves which makes for righteousness."[21] Mailer in *The Naked and the Dead* qualified Arnold's nineteenth-century affirmation of a natural moral order with a distinctively modern emphasis on the forces of life which, though not specifically moral, nevertheless impose some limits on the expression of absolute power.

Lieutenant Hearn and Red Valsen lack the single-minded pursuit of power of Croft and Cummings. Their goal is to maintain independent lives despite the presence of those who wish to mold them. Hearn is Mailer's study in the futility yet tragic heroism of liberal intellectualism. (In the historical allegory which runs through much of *The Naked and the Dead*, he and Valsen are the Lincoln Brigade, the mixture of college-bred and working-class Americans who fought for the Loyalist side against fascism during the Spanish Civil War.) Rebelling against his crass businessman father, but finding little of value in either left wing ideology or New York sophistication, Hearn is an isolato when he enters the army. His only aim in life (and in the army) is to maintain his "style" of personal freedom. But though he has said "I don't give a damn" to life (349), he also has an unacknowledged yearning to discover some meaning and direction in experience. In Cummings he finds an absorbing example of a man who in his commitment, single-mindedness, and incisiveness is everything Hearn believes he is not. His underlying responsiveness to these qualities is recognized by Cummings, and there follows an extended temptation narrative, as in three long interviews the general seeks to convince Hearn that Hearn shares his longing for power and thus his basic conception of life. These scenes, though ostensibly static discussions, in fact build toward a tense climax. We quickly realize that Cummings and Hearn are not merely talking about power but also living its reality in their personal relations—that Hearn resists the teachings of his mentor at the risk of his life.

Hearn's liberal sympathies lead him to condemn Cummings' Hobbesean view of man and the fascist philosophy of power which stems from it. But he also finds that certain aspects of a power philosophy—in particular the sheer animal pleasure of absolute control—attract him. He recalls a moment during a college pickup football game when he was about to make a tackle: "There had been an instant of complete startling gratification when he knew the ball carrier was helpless, waiting to be hit" (344). He realizes that Cummings is attempting to educate him in a "fear ladder" hatred and fear of Cummings and a contempt for the enlisted man. Ostensibly angry toward Cummings when he discovers this plan, but also frightened by his susceptibility to a power ethic, Hearn rebels by grinding a cigarette butt into the general's tent floor. Although Cummings is enraged by this rebellion by his star pupil, he also uses the incident to continue his instruction. Hearn's humiliation, as in a silent frenzy of fear and hate he is forced by Cummings to pick up the butt, completes both Hearn's education and the general's lesson. Afterwards Hearn muses: "Divorced of all the environmental trappings, all the confusing and misleading attitudes he had absorbed, he was basically like Cummings. . . . Cummings had been right. They were both the same, and it had produced first the intimacy, the attraction they had felt toward each other, and then the hatred" (392).

The patrol appears to confirm Hearn's bitter belief that his liberal attitudes were merely a disguise for his instinctive and suppressed love of power. At first, however, he responds to the challenge of Croft's effort to maintain his leadership of the platoon by seeking to cultivate in the men a sense of union in a joint enterprise. He wishes to command through mutual respect and camaraderie rather than by fear, hate, and contempt. But the platoon refuses to accept this form of leadership. As the fatigue and danger of the patrol increase, the men begin to view Hearn in the old way, as a focus of their hatred for what they are being forced to do. Hearn not only senses this feeling but also that the men prefer to be led by Croft. "Croft they would obey, for Croft satisfied their desire for hatred, encouraged it, was superior to it, and in turn exacted obedience" (506). A second confirmation of Cummings' teachings occurs in the first encounter of the patrol with the Japanese. Hearn's volition is frozen by the Japanese fire and he lies waiting for Croft to do something. But his realization that he has been expecting Croft to take command enrages him. As with Cummings and the cigarette butt, he senses, he is to be made a victim rather than an exploiter of fear. He assumes forceful command of the platoon, and in the successful completion of this act, as he leads the men back to safety, he discovers "an emotion . . . as sweet as anything he had ever known" (513). The final confirmation of Cummings' beliefs occurs in the incident of Croft killing the bird which Roth has found. Hearn forces Croft to apologize to Roth.

As Croft does so, Hearn realizes that he himself is playing the part, with some satisfaction, which Cummings played with him. He too is humiliating an underling and thereby breeding the hate and fear necessary for the maintenance of power.

That evening Hearn thinks through his experience on the patrol. He begins to sense the function of the patrol for him, that he doesn't care about its success or about the men "if he plumbed himself" (579). And this journey into the self has so far revealed the disconcerting truth that he desires the power of command both to "get a little of his own back from Cummings" (that is, gain Cummings' approval) and to experience its sheer pleasure, since leading the platoon has "become one of the most satisfying things he had ever done" (579, 580). Hearn's full and conscious acceptance of this aspect of himself brings a "shock [of] self-disgust" (580). A moral conflict is now clearly underway in Hearn between his animal delight in power and his rational recognition of its destructiveness. The focus of the conflict is whether to end the patrol because of the presence of the enemy and thus end his exercise in absolute power (on his side of the island he is comparable in power to Cummings on the other) or to continue it despite its increased dangers and its almost certain failure.

Hearn decides to return, but despite this decision he is tempted by Croft's suggestion that a man be sent to reconnoiter the pass ahead of them; if the Japanese have withdrawn, the patrol can continue. Martinez is sent and Hearn again takes up his internal debate. He now realizes that he must in the future place himself beyond the temptation of power and that a gesture in this direction would be to give up his commission on the return of the patrol. "It would be lousy and painful, and probably the only discovery would be that he could fit into a fear ladder as well as anyone else" (584). But he will do it nevertheless, both as a gesture and to prevent his becoming "another Croft." With this resolution, he can reject the teachings of Cummings:

> Cummings didn't know all the answers. If you granted him that man was a sonofabitch, then everything he said after that followed perfectly. The logic was inexorable.
>
> But the history wasn't. All right, all the great dreams had blunted and turned practical and corrupt, and the good things had often been done through bad motives, but still it

had not all been bad, there had also been victories where there should have been defeats. The world, by all the logics, should have turned Fascist and it hadn't yet. (585)

But the next morning, tricked by Croft's false report that the pass is free, Hearn is killed before he can translate his resolution into action.

Much of the negative criticism which Mailer's portrayal of Hearn has conventionally received stems from Mailer's difficulties in establishing a strong and convincing characterization of an intellectual without strong beliefs.[22] But much of this criticism also derives from a failure to recognize that Mailer grants Hearn only a limited victory and by no means depicts his final decision and death as a full triumph of the spirit. Hearn in his journey into himself acknowledges but does not fully control the "evil" which is the human yearning for power. This still lives and grows in him. Nor does Mailer suggest that Hearn's decision will really change the course of events. "Hearn and Quixote," Hearn thinks to himself (586). Nevertheless, only in the no doubt futile efforts of a Hearn, Mailer appears to be saying, is there any hope for mankind, given our natures. In an interview in 1948, Mailer said of *The Naked and the Dead*: "The book finds man corrupted, confused to the point of helplessness, but it also finds that there are limits beyond which he cannot be pushed, and it finds that even in his corruption and sickness there are yearnings for a better world."[23] Hearn's struggle against accepting that part of himself which Cummings and Croft believe to be inescapably central to man constitutes one of the "limits" which Mailer is dramatizing in *The Naked and the Dead*.

Although Red Valsen is from a radically different background than Hearn—born and raised in a poor mining town, he has spent his life at manual labor and on the move—he shares most of Hearn's essential characteristics and a portion of his fate. He is like Hearn in his contempt for the class structure of American life and in his fear of commitment or engagement. He too wishes to maintain an aloof independence because life has taught him the futility and dangers of involvement. Like Hearn, he cultivates an embittered isolation. " 'Nothing's worth a good goddamn,' " he says (233). Red is sought out by the weakest members of the platoon—Roth and Wyman, for example—because they sense his underlying compassion for those in difficulty. But in each instance he fights off open sympathy or involvement. His principal goal, like Hearn's, is to preserve his independence. "'I don't want to take no orders from nobody, and I don't want nobody to give 'em to me'" (445).

Red is able to fend off commitments and responsibilities (though one of the most experienced soldiers in the platoon, he resists being promoted to corporal), but he eventually finds—as did Hearn—that he cannot escape the fear ladder. Croft is his enemy, for Croft feels in Red an independence which threatens his power in the platoon. From the first day of the Anopopei invasion the two men confront each other in a series of near-violent incidents which derive from Red's belief that Croft must be opposed and Croft's sense that Red must be humiliated. Red believes that in a full show-down he will be able to outface Croft. But while climbing the mountain he realizes that he has been deluding himself, that he has absorbed the fear-ladder ethic of the army and that it is now part of him. "He had to face the truth. The Army had licked him. He had always gone along believing that if they pushed him around too much he would do something when the time came. And now . . ." (693). Red's final confrontation with Croft is therefore anti-climactic. Ordered by Croft to continue the climb, he gives in despite his realization of the futility and even madness of the effort (Roth has just died in a fall) and despite his recognition that with his lead the platoon might resist Croft: "He was licked. That was all there was to it. At the base of his shame was an added guilt. He was glad it was over, glad the long contest with Croft was finished, and he could obey orders with submission, without feeling that he must resist" (696).

Croft has won in this instance as he had with Hearn. Those who believe they can maintain their independence by opting out of the power structure are either destroyed by that structure or reabsorbed into it. But though Red survives and Hearn dies, Hearn is the stronger, which is why he must be killed and Red only humiliated. Nevertheless, like Hearn, Red has used the patrol to push through to a form of self-knowledge. On the boat trip back from the patrol, he muses:

> You carried it alone as long as you could, and then you weren't strong enough to take it any longer. You kept fighting everything, and everything broke you down, until in the end you were just a little goddamn bolt holding on and squealing when the machine went too fast.

He had to depend on other men, he needed other men now, and he didn't know how to go about it. Deep within him were the first nebulae of an idea, but he could not phrase it. If they all stuck together. . . . (703–4)

Both Hearn and Red have learned that they were not as "pure" and as "strong" as they thought they were; they could be corrupted and beaten. Hearn had reacted to this self-knowledge by making his gesture toward integrity; Red is beginning to struggle through to an understanding that man cannot survive alone. Both have been defeated but have nevertheless discovered alternatives to the fear ladder in their very defeat.

The patrol is also a journey into self for Croft. As portrayed by Mailer in the first portion of the novel, before the patrol, Croft is principally a figure parallel to Cummings in his desire to control men and events. Mailer's initial description of Croft in the Time Machine section devoted to him captures the machine-like destructiveness of the man:

> A lean man of medium height, but he held himself so erectly he appeared tall. His narrow triangular face was utterly without expression. There seemed nothing wasted in his hard small jaw, gaunt firm cheeks and straight short nose. His gelid eyes were very blue . . . he was efficient and strong and usually empty and his main cast of mind was a superior contempt toward nearly all other men. He hated weakness and he loved practically nothing. (156)

Yet Mailer ends this description with the cryptic comment: "There was a crude unformed vision in his soul but he was rarely conscious of it."

It is this unconscious, inarticulate, undefinable "vision" which comes to life in Croft's response to Mount Anaka during the patrol. When the patrol first glimpses the mountain, Croft above all is moved: "The mountain attracted him, taunted and inflamed him with its size. . . . He stared at it now, examined its ridges, feeling an instinctive desire to climb the mountain and stand at its peak. . . . His emotions were intense; he knew awe and hunger and [a] peculiar unique ecstasy" (447). Later, closer to the mountain, Croft refines this response. "Again, he felt a crude ecstasy. He could not have given the reason, but the mountain tormented him, beckoned him, held an answer to something he wanted. It was so pure, so austere" (497).

With the death of Hearn and with Croft's leadership of the platoon reestablished, the ascent of the mountain can begin. And now the significance of the taunting sexuality of the mountain for Croft becomes clearer as we sense that the climbing of Mount Anaka for him is a journey into the primitive, animal, instinctive center of himself—a journey through a wild, unexplored, and difficult landscape to the "pure" and "austere" absolute center of his identity. Croft undertakes this journey under the pressure of a compulsive desire, but he is also fearful, since its successful completion will result in the nakedness of complete self-knowledge. Croft, near the crest of the mountain,

> had been driving nearer and nearer to the heart of this country for days, and it had a cumulative terror. All the vast alien stretches of land they had crossed had eroded his will, pitched him a little finer. It was an effort, almost palpable, to keep advancing over strange hills and up the flanks of an ancient resisting mountain. For the first time in his life he started with fear every time an insect whipped into his face or an unnoticed leaf tickled his neck. . . . The mission of the patrol, indeed even the mountain, hardly moved him now. He progressed out of some internal contest in himself as if to see which pole of his nature would be successful. (699)

But the mountain—and Croft himself—remains inviolable and thus unknown. On the beach at the end of the patrol, Croft again views Mount Anaka and finds that "deep inside himself" he "was relieved that he had not been able to climb the mountain. For that afternoon at least, as the platoon waited . . . , Croft was rested by the unadmitted knowledge that he had found a limit to his hunger" (701). On the following day, as he sees the mountain for the last time before the patrol returns to its own lines, Croft relives both his hunger for conquest of the mountain and his relief at his failure:

> It was pure and remote. . . . The old torment burned in him again. A stream of wordless impulses beat in his throat and he had again the familiar and inexplicable tension the mountain always furnished him. To climb that.

... Once more he was feeling the anxiety and terror the
mountain had roused. ...

Croft kept looking at the mountain. He had lost it, had
missed some tantalizing revelation of himself.

Of himself and much more. Of life.

Everything. (709)

As a means toward revelation of self, Croft's effort to climb the
mountain is indeed analogous to Ahab's attempt to conquer Moby
Dick, as Mailer suggested in the 1951 interview in which he commented on his "mystic kick" in *The Naked and the Dead*. Of course,
Croft's view of the mountain is not the only possible one, just as
the whale has various meanings for different members of the *Pe-
quod* and for different ships. For Gallegher, raised in a Boston
slum, Mount Anaka is a vision of beauty (447), while Cummings
discovers in it something "bleak and alone, commanding the
heights" (563). Hearn finds its power and immensity frightening
(497). Mailer sought to suggest both the self-defining and the transcendent roles of the mountain in his 1948 interview when he commented that Mount Anaka meant "death and man's creative urge
and man's desire to conquer the elements, fate—all kinds of things
that you never dream of separating and stating so baldly."[24]

But to Croft the mountain is above all a means toward the definition of his strength, with the implication that in this knowledge
there is also knowledge of "everything." Like Ahab, Croft is obsessed by his quest, and thus what might have been a life-enhancing search for self-knowledge is a source of blindness and death.
Of course, Ahab destroys himself, while Croft destroys Hearn and
Roth and also maintains his place in the power structure. *The Naked and the Dead* is naturalistic fiction rather than fiction modeled
on Shakespearean tragedy, and in naturalism the symmetry of
high tragedy—of a fall to death—is often replaced by the anti-cli-
max of mixed and ambivalent conclusions. Power still rules in *The
Naked and the Dead* even though the human desire for absolute
knowledge and absolute control has been checked.

While the platoon has been struggling up the mountain, the litter-bearing detail of Ridges and Goldstein has been making its way
to the coast with the wounded Wilson. The detail initially includes
Stanley and Brown, but they soon drop out. Only the dull-witted
and good-natured Brooklyn Jew and the Arkansas dirt farmer
have the will to continue; the more worldly Stanley and Brown

quickly discover that it is to their advantage to lack the necessary strength. The journey of Goldstein and Ridges to the coast parallels Croft's symbolic journey to self-knowledge on the mountain. Here, too, the journey is unsuccessful both in the failure to complete the mission (Wilson dies enroute and even his body is swept away by a swift stream and is lost) and in what is revealed about oneself and life during the course of the journey. But here, too, the desire and ability of man to explore the depths of himself and of experience suggest a compensating transcendence in human nature whatever its other qualities and conditions.

Ridges and Goldstein have shared various duties and burdens throughout the invasion. They fought to keep their pup tent up during a tropical storm in the first portion of the novel, and they worked as a team cutting through the jungle early in the patrol. Underlying their sharing of tasks is a basic similarity of temperament. The two men are "doers" who accept the duties of life affirmatively and who push ahead as best they can in order to get the job done. They have an animal tenacity which gives them the strength to face the dilemmas and limitations of their marginal existence in the army as well as in civilian life. In both men, temperament is bolstered by faith—the primitive protestant religiosity and work ethic of Ridges, the Jewish will to survive of Goldstein. Indeed, Mailer suggests in Ridges an extension into the Arkansas farmer of the Jewish capacity to suffer and endure. Goldstein recalls his grandfather's definition of a Jew—"a Jew is a Jew because he suffers. . . . We have suffered so much that we know how to endure" (483)—a definition which helps give him the strength to put "his face to the wind" (492) and thus survive in the army, just as the degradation and poverty yet sustaining religiosity of Ridges' farm background have given him a reservoir of forebearance and strength.

The litter-bearing detail is not a sentimental exercise on the theme of men establishing a communion of effort and purpose through the compassionate nature of their enterprise. The bearers are bound to each other not in charity but "in an unwilling union of exhaustion and rage" (622)—rage at Wilson and at each other. Nor do they have a conscious awareness of the implications of their journey. Their burden reduces them "to the lowest common denominator of their existence. Carrying him was the only reality they knew" (644). Nevertheless, both for us and for Ridges and Goldstein the journey gradually becomes a symbolic journey closely related to the religious experience familiar to each. To the Christian, the detail takes on the character of an exemplum from *The Pilgrim's Progress*, while the Jew begins to identify with Wilson's pain, a pain which "slowly, keeping pace with his exhaustion, . . . had entered his own body" (668). Ridges dimly perceives that the detail

> meant something else; they were being taught by example or maybe they were paying for their own sins. Ridges did not work it out for himself, but it gave him a mixture of dread and the variety of exultation that comes with too much fatigue. (671)

As for Goldstein,

> His senses dammed, his consciousness reeling, Goldstein fumbled through a hall of symbols. Wilson was the object he could not release. Goldstein was bound to him by a fear he did not understand. If he let him go, if he did not bring him back, then something was wrong, he would understand something terrible. . . . There was a meaning here and Goldstein lumbered after it. . . . (673)

Ridges and Goldstein, as each searches in his own way for the symbolic meaning of his pain and exhaustion, begin to sense that their journey is a life allegory—that life itself is a journey in pain and anger and exhaustion and that it too will end in failure, in death. Both now realize the immense burdens they have carried through life—the marginal farmer as drudge, the Jew as universal scapegoat—and that theirs is indeed a painful and exhausting journey with no possible relief other than death. But despite this realization Ridges and Goldstein continue the detail under a terrible compulsion to see the journey through, to reach full self-knowledge even though they bitterly anticipate what this knowledge will be. And they are not disappointed in that anticipation. Wilson, the wounded man who has become an extension of themselves, dies and his body is swept away; they arrive at the beach empty-handed. They feel openly now the immense unfairness and injustice of life, that men should struggle so hard and yet achieve nothing. Ridges curses and weeps:

He had carried this burden through such distances of space and time, and it had washed away in the end. All his life he had labored without repayment. . . . Ridges felt the beginning of a deep and unending bitterness. It was not fair. . . . He wept out of bitterness and longing and despair; he wept from exhaustion and failure and the shattering naked conviction that nothing mattered. (681–82)

And Goldstein, still identifying Wilson with the burden which all Jews carry, thinks that

all the suffering of the Jews came to nothing. No sacrifices were paid, no lessons were learned. It was all thrown away, all statistics in the cruel wastes of history. All the ghettos, all the soul cripplings, all the massacres and pogroms, the gas chambers, lime kilns—all of it touched no one, all of it was lost. It was carried and carried and carried, and when it finally grew too heavy it was dropped. . . . There was nothing in him at the moment, nothing but a vague anger, a deep resentment, and the origins of a vast hopelessness. (682)[25]

Croft in his journey into self had found a frustrating limit to his power; Ridges and Goldstein in their journey discover the emptiness and hopelessness of their struggle through life. But despite the devastating nature of this self-knowledge, it nevertheless is self-knowledge. Man can face the outer edges of experience and of himself and seek to strike through, in exhaustion and rage, to the truth about himself and life; he can attempt to be a seer. And if this knowledge reveals the existential truth of the amoral emptiness of life, it also affirms and endorses the existential morality of the honest and concrete testing of the limits of life and of self, whatever the cost.

The platoon as a group in *The Naked and the Dead* appears to reflect a number of clichéd themes in the depiction of lower-class secondary characters in the naturalistic novel. Besides their obvious grossness and vulgarity, they have all been shaped by their peacetime worlds into patterns of frustration, bitterness, and meanness which are expressed in shallowness of spirit and insight. Their humor is clumsy, their allegiances momentary, and their energies are directed principally toward survival. We encounter them in the major events of "Argil and Mold"—the storm, the anti-tank gun detail, and the river fire-fight—in a setting of unending heat, wetness, and decay. They sweat and struggle like beasts of burden under the anti-tank guns, and they cringe in fear and terror under enemy fire. They are the "mass" in its least attractive form—the clay to be molded and often discarded by those of greater power, knowledge, and skill. Their importance in the larger scheme of things is summed up by Red's remark that "'A man's no more important than a goddamn cow'" (199).

The platoon is a "class" as well as an "animal" construct. Mailer gives each of its members a distinctive local background, but in fact it is the class rather than geographical nature of this background which is the determining factor in each character's make-up and condition. Martinez seeks any form of acceptance because he is a Mexican-American; Pollack, Minetta, and Gallegher are belligerently shrewd, slum-bred, first generation Americans; Wilson and Ridges are poor white; and Brown and Stanley are beleaguered by lower middle class anxieties and fears.

The Time Machine sections in *The Naked and the Dead* are principally a superficial exercise in the 1930s naturalistic theme of man as a creature of class. These sections (all of which, with the exception of those on Hearn and Cummings, are devoted to the enlisted men of the platoon) have been rightly criticized as the weakest fictional element in the novel. They are derivative both in their general character as impressionistic biography combining features of Dos Passos' biographies and Steinbeck's interchapters and in the specific borrowings within individual portraits. (Wilson leans heavily on Erskine Caldwell, Gallegher on Farrell, Brown on Sinclair Lewis, Red on Dos Passos, Pollack on the 1930s gangster film, and so on.) In addition, the Time Machine portraits communicate a stereotyped social determinism with insufficient individuality of characterization for either symbolism or satire. We merely feel that we have encountered the circumstances of this life many times before.[26] Only Goldstein's Time Machine has life, since in this instance Mailer sketches a background he knows well and also creates a figure who in fact is an anomaly in his world.

Mailer's depiction of the platoon as a dramatic presence on the island, however, is a far more effective representation of his underlying notions about its members than are his blatantly schematic Time Machine sections. Wilson's Time Machine, for example, presents us with a pleasure-seeking irresponsible poor white. His desire to have "a little fun" (378) regardless of cost to himself and others is caricature without bite or point. But in his interaction with the platoon Wilson's character comes alive. Now the shrewd self-interest beneath his apparently easygoing naiveté (as in the liquor purchasing incident) adds complexity to the portrait, and now his raucous youth—as recalled in his delirious reveries just after being shot and later on the litter—contributes to a moving tension between present pain and remembered pleasure. The Time Machines, in short, present us with types, the rendered experience of the platoon creates compelling individuals.

As we come to know the men of the platoon in the course of the novel, we discover in them the naturalistic attributes of a suppressed core of sensibility and understanding beneath the shapes forced upon them by their backgrounds and condition. An example of this quality in the platoon as a whole occurs during the sea voyage to the south side of Anopopei at the beginning of the patrol. A tropical sunset illuminates the horizon, creating for a moment a beautiful sensual world. The men "responded to it with an acute and terrible longing. It was a vision of all the beauty for which they had ever yearned, all the ecstasy they had ever sought. For a few minutes it dissolved the long dreary passage of the mute months in the jungle, without hope, without pride" (454). But the sun goes down, leaving the dark sea. "The black dead ocean looked like a mirror of the night; it was cold, implicit with dread and death" (454). The moment sums up the lives of the men of the platoon—a transient perception of beauty within the permanent setting of blackness, both in life and in death. The mood is that of pathos because a basic human capacity is so seldom fulfilled and thus so seldom relieves the essential bleakness of life.

Mailer plays upon the naturalistic irony of the presence of sensibility in even the most contemptible figure in the platoon. Gallegher is his fullest and most paradigmatic exercise in this form of irony. Deeply resentful toward life because he "never had a fuggin break" (201), Gallegher is racked by self-pity and reaches out for someone to blame. In his ignorance and hatreds he is the bedrock on which a fascist state can be erected. Yet in the lengthy incident in which Gallegher receives and gradually absorbs the news of the death of his wife in childbirth, we respond to the genuineness of his loss and pain and to the depth of his suffering. When he finally accepts that his wife is dead, "He heard himself sob, and then was no longer conscious of the choking sounds of his anguish. He felt only a vast grief which mellowed him, dissolved the cysts of his bitterness and resentment and fear, and left him spent and weeping on the sand" (285). In his suffering Gallegher achieves an element of dignity and emotional honesty. He is still the same contemptible Jew-baiting figure afterwards, but we know that he is something more than this as well.

The same rounding and deepening occurs with other characters. Minetta, a figure of almost despicable self-pity and ineptitude, glows with a tragic nostalgia for the peace and stability of the small Italian town where he was born. Martinez, whose fawning dependence on Croft contributes to Hearn's death, feels a great pang of wrongness and self-loathing at the human waste when he is forced to kill a Japanese sentry; and Roth, the least capable soldier in the platoon, has his moment of tragic manhood on the mountain when he brings himself to confront and oppose Croft. These are men who are frustrated and tormented and controlled by the power structure of life both in and outside the army, but they are "men for all that," Mailer seems to be saying, in the yearning or suffering or understanding or courage which they are able to express. It was perhaps this dual character of the platoon which led Mailer in 1951 to tell an interviewer that a writer "has to be capable of knowing the rot, and he has to be able to strip it down to the stink, but he also has to love that rot."[27]

This emotional ambivalence is central to the power and effect of *The Naked and the Dead*. In the major tradition of naturalistic fiction in America, Mailer offers a vision of life neither as fully conditioned nor as lacking all value. This pervasive quality in the novel as a whole can perhaps best be illustrated by examples from a few significant passages and scenes. One such example is Mailer's use of the term "sonofabitch" in relation to the human condition. During the platoon's climb of the mountain, Wyman asks Polack, a man of fundamental animal shrewdness, if he thinks there is a God. Angry and frustrated by the climb—in other words, embittered by his position on the fear ladder—Polack replies, "'If there is, he sure is a sonofabitch'" (607). But Hearn, in the evening before his death when he has decided to make his gesture of resistance to the fear ladder by resigning his commission, thinks to himself, "Cummings didn't know all the answers. If you granted him that man was a sonofabitch, then everything he said after that followed perfectly." But in fact, Hearn continues, there had been some "great dreams" and some "good things" and some "victories" to dispute Cummings' assumption (585). God and his creation, man, may appear to be "sonofabitches" and indeed often are; but there is also evidence to the contrary.

Something of the same ambivalence characterizes the state of the platoon after the patrol. From Croft downward the platoon is exhausted and dismayed. The mountain had not been conquered, and Hearn and Roth had died in vain, since the island had been secured independently of the mission of the patrol. And the future offers little comfort. "They were still on the treadmill; the misery, the ennui, the dislocated horror. . . . Things would happen and time would pass, but there was no hope, no anticipation. There would be nothing but the deep cloudy dejection that overcast everything" (702). Yet despite this sense of futility, of life as empty and meaningless, there are glimmers among several of the men of something now understood and therefore gained from their experience—something in particular, as in *The Red Badge of Courage*, about the nature of group enterprises and of the union of men under pressure. Red senses in his weariness and defeat that "He had to depend on other men, he needed other men now. . . . Deep within him were the first nebulae of an idea" (704). And Goldstein now thinks, "He had a buddy. . . . There was an understanding between Ridges and him. The day they had been spent on the beach waiting for the rest of the platoon had not been unpleasant. And automatically they had selected bunks next to each other when they got on the boat" (704). And even the isolated and proud Croft reflects on the role of the platoon in his effort to climb the mountain. "If he had gone alone, the fatigue of the other men would not have slowed him but he would not have had their company, and he realized suddenly that he could not have gone without them. The empty hills would have eroded any man's courage" (709). A necessary and occasionally rewarding interdependence between the individual and the group is thus both affirmed in the events of the patrol and depicted as a realization in the minds of some of its participants. Life, in short, can be understood as well as suffered. The platoon may be clay to be molded, but man can journey both toward self-knowledge and toward a measure of self-determination even in defeat.

William Styron

Lie Down in Darkness

William Styron's first novel, published in 1951 when he was twenty-six, is as obviously indebted to Faulkner as was Mailer's *The Naked and the Dead* to Dos Passos and Farrell. The presence in a novel with a Southern setting of a family consisting in part of a weak father, shrewish mother, and doomed daughter, of a journey with a coffin, of a richly poetic prose and a fractured narrative style, to say nothing of a host of more specific Faulknerian echoes—all suggested a youthful disciple who had produced a derivative homage rather than an original work. Criticism of *Lie Down in Darkness* has always been preoccupied with the Faulknerian or Southern characteristics of the novel.[1] How much in Styron's novel is explainable (and thus, it is implied, limited) by the specifically regional in theme and form, and how much of it is an independent work of art? Styron has himself been as sensitive to this issue as have been his critics. He has always acknowledged the powerful influence of Faulkner on his early writing, but he has also insisted that he was affected equally by other major writers (Melville and Dostoevsky, for example)[2] and that *Lie Down in Darkness* has its own distinctive character. He told an interviewer in 1951 that he wished in *Lie Down in Darkness* to avoid both "the ancestral theme" and "the old idea of wreckage and defeat as a peculiarly Southern phenomenon. Elements of this are in the book, but they're part of the people rather than the place."[3] And in 1959 he noted that "I would like to believe that my people would have behaved the way they did anywhere."[4]

Efforts by Styron and some of his critics to disassociate the principal impact of *Lie Down in Darkness* from its Southern setting have often merely resulted in pigeonholing of another kind. If the novel is not about the decay of the South, it must be about the dissolution of modern life. Touching most of the bases of the current idea of modernity, one critic has noted the "existential atmosphere" of a novel in which characters hover "between a drugged conventionality . . . and a terror of the meaninglessness of existence."[5] *Lie Down in Darkness* is set in the late 1930s and early 1940s, and ends in August 1945, with the suicide of Peyton Loftis and the spiritual death of her parents, Helen and Milton Loftis. Styron accompanies this study in the collapse of a middle-class family with allusions to Nazi death camps (in Helen's nightmare of a decaying city of the dead) and with explicit references to the dropping of the atomic bomb on Nagasaki, an event which occurs on the day of Peyton's suicide. The novel also includes a gratuitous passage which explains that the function of the artist in "perilous times such as ours"[6] is to paint pictures similar to Harry's, in which an old man in a ruined city looks "proudly upward" for an answer to the human dilemma represented by mass destruction.[7]

Both of these approaches to *Lie Down in Darkness*—as a Faulknerian Southern novel and as a "contemporary statement"—offer considerable insight into the work. But oddly neglected as a major approach to *Lie Down in Darkness* is its character as a naturalistic novel, and in particular as a novel in which the metaphor of a troubled journey through life is used to explore the naturalistic question of our responsibility for our fates. The novel also fulfills Frank Norris's definition of naturalism as fiction in which seemingly commonplace characters are "twisted from the ordinary, wrenched out from the quiet, uneventful round of every-day life, and flung into the throes of a vast and terrible drama."[8] *Lie Down in Darkness* presents us not with extraordinary characters in extraordinary circumstances but rather with an "average" middle-class family of some wealth and position. The Loftises are not the victims of major flaws in their heredity and environment; they need only flow in the grooved paths which their class has prepared for them. Yet their lives move toward chaos and death, toward the "Nothing" which Milton and Helen shout at each other over their daughter's coffin.[9] As Milton realizes, in an explanation which has resonance for the novel as a whole, even such an occasion as Peyton's wedding can disintegrate into fear, anger, and hate and is thus not "a commonplace and civilized social event but a nightmare in vivid technicolor" (306).

It is conventional in discussions of *Lie Down in Darkness* to note the Freudian nature of the family triangle in the novel.[10] Indeed, even Milton and Peyton refer to it on several occasions (76, 235). A more useful and provocative comment,. however, is Maxwell Geismar's observation that Styron renders the Electra complex in *Lie Down in Darkness* with "such brilliant and intuitive and natural Freudian insights as to be completely non-Freudian."[11] Geismar is here suggesting, I think, that the sexual neuroses of the Loftises are communicated to us not as a Freudian formulation but rather as products of deeply ingrained weaknesses of character, and that Styron has thus convinced us of the validity of his characterization rather than of the truth of Freud's theory. This effect is of course cumulative; we know more about the characters at the end of the novel than we do during its early portions, and our attitude changes from initial thin sympathy for Helen as a put-down wife and minor irritation toward Milton as a self-indulgent philanderer to final compassion for Milton and heartfelt repugnance toward Helen. Nevertheless, the basic nature of each of the major characters is fully revealed in specific scenes of what can be called "negative epiphany"—scenes in which the self discovers in a moment of insight not the wonder and beauty and unity of life but rather the emptiness of existence and the isolation of the spirit. Two brief but significant moments in the novel are devoted to introducing the early history of the family triangle, while three far more extended scenes of negative epiphany reveal the essential character of each of the figures in the triangle.

Our first awareness of the tensions within the Loftis family—in simplest terms, of Milton's selfish possessiveness, Peyton's futile resistance, and Helen's jealousy—occurs in Helen's memory, early in the novel, of an incident in Peyton's childhood. Peyton had run from a swarm of bees,

> *Why the Dear,* [Helen] thought, *she wandered up there all by herself,* and warm, shivery, she arose, her arms outstretched— *why, my dearest baby*—but Milton was running from his chair, intercepting her, tossing Peyton high in the air. . . . And so, nuzzling his face against her neck, he bore her toward the porch. . . . Helen sat down again. The coffee on her breakfast tray was suddenly without taste, and for a moment she felt a helpless frustration. (29)

A parallel moment occurs somewhat later in Peyton's childhood, when she and Milton (as recalled by Milton during Peyton's wedding) climb a church bell tower and Peyton is frightened by the chimes:

> He lifts her to the ledge and puts his arm about her, telling her not to be frightened. Beneath the eaves sparrows scuttle in their nests and fly off with a raucous sound. . . . He doesn't know why his heart pounds so nor, when he kisses her again, in an agony of love, why she should push him so violently away with her warm small hands. (290)

These scenes of explicit Freudianism are, however, only the outward expression of a deep malaise of character and spirit of each of the figures, a malaise which is disclosed in their extended scenes of self-revelation.

Milton is fully revealed to us, and to himself, during a November day in Charlottesville in 1942. All the Loftises are in the city—Helen and Maudie (the Loftises' retarded child) at a hospital, Peyton (who is now nineteen) to attend a football game, and Milton because he has been called by Helen when she has learned that Maudie is seriously ill. Milton at this point in his life is jaded and dissatisfied. In this humor, and drinking heavily (as he has done for many years), he realizes that he is not an alcoholic, "only self-indulgent, and his disease, whatever it was, resided in shadier corners of his soul—where decisions were reached not through reason but by rationalization, and where a thin membranous growth of selfishness always seemed to prevent his decent motives from becoming happy actions" (152–53). The events of the day dramatize the consequences of Milton's lifelong habit of emotional selfishness and moral evasiveness. During a visit to the hospital he realizes that Helen has used Maudie as a refuge and that Maudie's death will strengthen and redirect her jealous hate toward himself and Peyton. Later he meets the former husband of his mistress Dolly and is reminded of the tawdriness and superficiality of his affair with her. Finally, he is unsuccessful in his efforts to find Peyton and also learns that she has just been "pinned." One love has ended in hate, another was never more than a shallow indulgence, and the last and deepest not only cannot be fully acknowledged but is lost. So Milton does what he has done all his life when presented with disappointments and dilemmas—he gets drunk and hides, hides on this occasion by going to the football game, where, while idiotically waving a Confederate flag, "his conscience, reviving from the brown depths of the day, told him that it was true: sitting here evading all, evading his very identity among people for whom that fact, at least, was of no importance, he had committed the unpardonable sin. It was neither one of commission nor of omission, but the worst combination of both—of apathy, of a sottish criminal inertia" (209).

A parallel full revelation of Helen's character occurs during the longest and most powerful scene of the novel, the wedding of Peyton and Harry in December 1943. Ostensibly Helen is now at peace. After Maudie's death a contrite and indeed emasculated Milton had returned to her under her terms, and Peyton—who had broken with her even before Charlottesville—has "made up" and has permitted the wedding to occur at home. The wedding is to be Helen's triumph—the public display of the formerly errant husband and wayward daughter who have at last admitted her greater wisdom and accepted her pardon and guidance. So she "struggle[s] to accomplish [the] casual, collected air of the proud mother: the woman who has sacrificed, whose suffering is known to the community, but who, on the day of her daughter's marriage, presents only the face of humility and courage and gentle good will" (273). It is a "struggle" for Helen to play this role because she is in fact moved by the bitterest jealousy. Peyton's return has reunited her with Milton, and this inspires in Helen an even more virulent form of the self-absorbed and sadistic moralism which had characterized most of her life with Milton. When he had returned to her after Charlottesville, she had taken pleasure in "the chance to watch him plead and grovel and humiliate himself. What more, for one who had suffered a lifetime of indignities, of so much emotional privation, could be asked?" (273) Peyton's return, however, has freed Milton from this role and has also resulted in the public display of the love between father and daughter. Helen therefore adopts a conscious Iago-like demeanor: her "genteel sprightliness masked the most villainous intentions," a desire to give shape and expression to her "profound and unalterable *loathing* of Peyton" (274).

And so the operative ethic of Helen's life stands fully revealed as a core of hate, jealousy, and vengeance masked by a series of moralistic roles. She unsuccessfully tries, after she has worked herself into a frenzy of self-righteousness, to explain herself to Carey Carr, the liberal-minded Episcopal clergyman who has been attempting to help her for many years. But what does he know, she asks herself, "of a woman like herself—despised, rejected, but always patient, reveling in the violent surge of the blood—whose dreams were always crowded with enemies" (297). Carey senses Helen's paranoia and tells her that she is "a very sick woman," and later, when she expresses fully her hatred for Peyton, that she is "mad" (295, 300). The drunken Milton offers another perspective on Helen after she calls Peyton a whore. "'God help you, you monshter,'" he cries (312).

We come to know Peyton most fully at the close of the novel through her lengthy interior monologue on the day of her death. Earlier we have glimpses of her appealing self-honesty and wry humor as well as of her thwarted search for a "normal" life. But on the day of her death, as she makes love to the milkman Tony, looks for her estranged husband Harry, and travels to Harlem to leap from a seventh floor window, she reveals herself directly and completely. As befits an interior monologue devoted to a disturbed mind, she speaks to us most of all through the obsessive images and symbols which populate her consciousness—her desire to escape into the dark timeless womb of the interior of a clock from the birds and chimes she associates with a forbidden sexuality which also threatens to drown her. ("All hope lies beyond memory," she had told an analyst, "back in the slick dark womb" [372].) Within the clock she will be safe from the oppressive sexuality of her adulthood and particularly of the immediate present—Tony taking her despite her menstrual cramps, the soldier attempting to pick her up in the bar, the heat of the day. There she will find both purity and protection. Life for her has been increasingly a desperate effort to purge her dependent love for Milton by sex with other men. But the failure of this effort ("for once I awoke, half-sleeping, and pulled away. 'No Bunny,' I said" [377].) and the failure to win back Harry, who was to accompany her into the clock, impel her to return instead to the purity of childhood. Even her prayers are heavily colored by this desire: "Lighten my darkness, I beseech you, oh Lord, and make me clean and pure and without sin, . . . make me as I was when I was a child" (359). God to her is neither a Christian God nor a God of nature—"I would not pray to a polyp or a jellyfish, nor to Jesus Christ"—but a God of innocence, "that part of me that was pure and lost now, when [Milton] and I used to walk along the beach, toward Hampton, and pick up shells" (368). But escape into the past is impossible except by obliterating the present, and so Peyton strips herself "naked, clean . . . just as

I had come" (386) and plunges to her death. She has lain down in darkness because she desires, as the second epigraph to the novel puts it, to be carried "along, taddy, like you done through the toy fair."

Milton, Helen, and Peyton form a triangle of desperate attachment without communion, of emotional over-dependence and exploitation which produces a paradoxical isolation of the spirit. Circling this triangle are figures who appear to offer some relief for the oppressive and destructive emotions within it but who in fact fail to do so. Maudie, Dolly, and Harry are ineffectual substitutes outside the triangle for the love each member seeks within it. Dolly offers all that Helen doesn't—"rapt adoration," "mindless constancy," and a vanity-flattering submissiveness (43). Maudie, in her permanent childishness, will never rebel, as Peyton had done, and she also permits Helen to focus all her passion on a sexless relationship. And Harry, whom Peyton wants to marry because she needs him, is a father surrogate. But Dolly is vacuous, Maudie is an unresponsive reflector of Helen's love, and Harry cannot accept the role which Peyton wishes him to play.

Heavenly love is equally useless to the Loftises in their search for relief. Formal "high" religion is represented by the uninspired, thin-blooded, and skeptical religiosity of Carey Carr, "low" folk religion by the primitive emotionalism (as well as charlatanism) of Daddy Faith. But neither can reach those in need. Peyton and Helen remain locked in private worlds in which their obsessions lead to a mouthing of religious formulations rather than to an acceptance of religious truth. Daddy Faith's promise of "peace, redemption, [and] the cleansing of the sea" (102) may produce in Ella Swan, the Loftises' black servant, "a perfect peace, a transcendent understanding" (396); but to the Loftises on their way to the cemetery Daddy Faith's revival meeting is a cause of traffic congestion rather than a potential resource. For Peyton there is no transcendent father and no redemption, and there is no cleansing except in obliteration. And for Helen and Milton there is no faith; there is only "Nothing."

Styron's symmetry of characterization in *Lie Down in Darkness* (a triangle surrounded by balanced but unsatisfactory alternative commitments) is matched by his division of the form of the novel into two parallel double journeys. It is this narrative strategy which is responsible for much of the holding power of the novel as fiction. In each of the double journeys a physical movement through space (Helen and Milton taking Peyton's body to the cemetery, Peyton searching for Harry on her last day alive) is accompanied by a journey into the past as the principal characters plumb their memories for the meaning of their lives. And in each of the double journeys, the characters seek unavailingly to reverse the passage of time, to recover what they believe they possessed in the past. The novel thus generates great density of feeling through its constant interplay of past and present. A character's past pain is also felt as it is relived in the present, present pain seeks its origin in the past, and so highly charged emotions feed upon each other from the first moment of *Lie Down in Darkness* to its conclusion.

The principal double journey is that of Milton and Helen on a hot August day of 1945 as Milton and Dolly Bonner accompany Peyton's body from the Port Warwick dock to the cemetery while Helen and Carey Carr make their way there independently from the Loftis home. In the course of the day the Loftises relive their lives, through reverie and recollection, from their youth and marriage to the climactic debacle of Peyton's wedding in December 1943. Styron's use of a free-association technique to move fluidly backwards and forwards in time—a thought or impression in the present triggers a recollection of the past—at first appears to be largely a device to ease narrative transitions. It also, however, contributes to the representation of the isolation of his major figures. As each pursues his understanding of the present by means of his recollection of the past, he projects through his memories both a dramatic and a personal vision of experience; he frequently describes not so much "reality" as his own limited understanding both of himself and of the moment he is recalling. *Lie Down in Darkness* thus often achieves the effect of what can be called epistemological tragedy—our responsiveness to the anguish of a character is combined with our recognition that he fails to understand the roots of his suffering even while attempting to do so. In an example of this theme at its most obvious, Dolly's ruminations about Milton late in their affair reveal principally her own painfully fatuous hopes about the relationship rather than an understanding either of herself or Milton: "She loved him so much when he was sober, which was fairly infrequent; then his very spirit, so uncompromisingly aware of life, of the poignancy of their dilemma, so richly conscious of the fine things soon in store for them—this sober, gentle spirit promised to envelop her like a flame, a tender flame radiating decent contentment" (72–73).

Peyton's wedding brings to a horrendous conclusion the tendency of the major characters to see or respond to life almost entirely from the perspective of an obsessed private vision. Milton's sexual torment and longing, Helen's dishonesty and loathing, Peyton's panicky desire for "normality"—each provides a distorting lens for the occasion while simultaneously focusing clearly on the interior life of the viewer. At one point earlier in the novel, during a typical moment of crossed feelings among Peyton, Milton, and Helen, Milton thinks "If [Helen] knew what was true, if I knew what truth was too, we could love each other" (96). But in fact neither can know what truth is, as Milton himself unconsciously reveals in his self-pitying remark, since in every instance limitations of character blur understanding. Styron appears to be saying that the truth which each person seeks about himself is inevitably solipsistic because it serves his own ends—self-pity for Milton, pride for Helen—rather than the goal of disinterested accuracy.

Nevertheless, because we experience most of the major moments in the novel through more than one perspective, and because these moments also contain much that we presume to be true because of an assumed accuracy in the recollection of dialogue, we do emerge with a sense of specific scenes not only as a reflection of particular limited understandings but as actual events. Also, although we move backwards and forwards in time within a scene, the "big" scenes depicting the dissolution of the Loftises maintain a rough chronological progression within the novel as a whole. These scenes are middle-class family occasions—weekends, holidays, birthdays, and weddings—which presume family unity but which for the Loftises always erupt in explosions of anger, bitterness, and hate. These major occasions punctuate the novel and lend it much of its internal rhythm. We begin with a Sunday lawn gathering when Peyton is nine and proceed to her sixteenth birthday party, to the Charlottesville visit during a football weekend, to Peyton's wedding. As we become attuned to these scenes we accept their own internal structure of associational shifts in time using several perspectives and we respond to the almost painful expectation of disaster that is their internal emotional rhythm—that what should be a ritualized occasion of middle class contentment and fulfillment is proceeding toward and will eventually reach a nightmare of frustration and anger.

The Loftises often seek to overcome the conflicts generated by the family triangle and occasionally appear to do so. These moments of hope and reconciliation are followed by even sharper descents into a chaos of destructive emotions. Thus the pattern of events in the novel is of a character precipitating a disaster by an act of rebellion or pride or selfishness and then seeking reconciliation but the very effort at reconciliation impelling the family forward into yet another disaster. Peyton, when she is punished by Helen, seeks comfort from Milton, which only embitters Helen further. Milton, when he returns to Helen, must be punished and humiliated for his "sins," which lays the foundation for his next rebellion. Perhaps the key metaphor for the Loftises' passage through life is contained in Helen's recurrent dream of Milton coming to her at night seeking a reconciliation. Helen, in her dream, remains silent, even while thinking,

> Oh I want to love him. I do. Again. He left her without a sound. And as he left, in this familiar reverie, so real, yet somehow airy and strange, she collapsed back into bed, or rather into absolute darkness, knowing that by one word— Yes or Forgive or Love—she might have affirmed all, released all of the false and vengeful and troubling demons up into the encompassing air of night, and everything would be right again. But she fell back into darkness. (82)

It is not Peyton alone who lies down in darkness. All the Loftises throughout the novel continually fall back into the darkness of their private and self-destructive isolation of spirit.

Helen in her dream and Milton elsewhere frequently speak of the love they wish to recapture through reconciliation. But it is clear that their longing for a renewal of love is similar to Peyton's desire to return to the innocence of childhood. They mean by "love" an emotion which exists apart from the tensions and pressures of adulthood, an emotion which has the peace, simplicity, and purity that one might attribute to children in love. The recovery of love to Helen and Milton is thus a form of nostalgia, of mining out of the past an emotion encrusted with the remembered trappings of romance. Milton unconsciously reveals this notion when he attempts to explain to Peyton the love that exists between Helen and himself,

a love which had been held together by the merest wisp of
music, faintly heard only during unwitting moments when
memory washed at their minds like breakers against crum-
bling stones; a love in which the principals involved might
have dwelt at opposite rims of the universe, only to be
drawn back always by some force he could never define—
the impalpable, thin strand of music, a memory of lost, en-
folding arms, or the common recollection of a happening
very ordinary, but which had happened to them together—
these and all the gardenias and roses, ruined scents that
hovered in the air so many years ago, in the grass-green
light of another dawn. (267)

For Styron in *Lie Down in Darkness* love in the present is pain and
conflict; only in its remembered innocence—or in the permanent
innocence of a Maudie, in her love for the conjurer—can it be
anything else.

Peyton's wedding seems to the Loftises to be an opportunity to
escape from the emotions which have shaped their lives. They are
temporarily reconciled and the future appears bright. But this
long scene, which is almost Shakespearean in structure and texture
(the disguised feelings and motives of the principal figures, the
constant shifting of characters into new groups within a forward-
moving action, the mingling of farce and tragedy, the lyric prose),
again ends in the familiar chaos of hate. It also ends the journey
through the past which is to conclude in the "present" of the fu-
neral. Although the wedding occurs a year and a half before Peyton's death, it has brought her life to its "logical" conclusion of
recognition of her absolute hate of her mother and her insoluble
love for her father. Thus, at a moment of seeming "beginning"—
as she and her husband cross the ferry to Norfolk to start their
honeymoon—she is drawn by the oblivion which the waters of the
bay appear to offer. " 'It *is* dark and lovely,' " she says (321).

The ferry crossing is an apt symbol of the conclusion of Peyton's
troubled crossing through life, since it is at the station dock a year
and a half later that the "present" journey of Milton and Helen
begins as Milton awaits the arrival of the train bearing Peyton's
corpse.[12] This journey also has its internal cycle of initial hope culminating in despair and emptiness. Peyton's trust that she will lie
down in darkness to rise in innocence is matched by the conventional Christian belief of Carey Carr, who is accompanying Helen,

and by Daddy Faith ("Happy am I in my Redeemer" [104]), whose revival meeting is crowding the route. The journey also begins with a thread of desperate hope for this life, since Milton expects to achieve during the day a reconciliation with Helen, from whom he has been separated since the wedding. He will, he thinks as he waits for the train, "cure her, make her well, tell her that our love never went away at all" (36).[13] Carey Carr is also committed to this goal because of his belief that Milton and Helen need each other. The journey to the cemetery is thus yet another typical Loftis family moment—the family together at an important occasion and beginning it in hope for unity, love, and peace. But the journey is more than a repetition of the major scenes in the life of the Loftises which end in disaster; it also so cruelly mocks the vacuousness and fatuousness of their hopes that we almost welcome the "red flash of violence" (388) which concludes it and which symbolizes the permanent division between Milton and Helen.

Styron suggests the triteness of Milton's hopes at the very onset of the journey when a jukebox in the dock lunch room blares forth the refrain "Take me back and try me one more time" (41). But his basic device for the representation of the emptiness of the Loftises' expectations is the ironic similarity between their journey and that in T. S. Eliot's "The Waste Land." The trip to the cemetery passes through a modern industrial wasteland of polluted marshland and urban neglect and decay, of garbage dumps with their rats and odors, of desolate filling stations, and of gas storage tanks "rising up out of the wasteland" (69). But at last the two cars and the hearse pass through this symbolic equivalent of the lives of the Loftis family and reach the cemetery chapel, the "chapel perilous" of the conclusion of Eliot's poem when the thunder speaks its message of hope of rain and rebirth. Now, too, there is thunder and an August downpour, and now, too, there is hope. Helen had seemed to be "compliant," Carey Carr had told Milton that "'You've got salvation in your hands almost'" (243), and so Milton seeks a reconciliation. But instead of cleansing and regeneration, instead of the giving, sympathy, and control which the thunder had advised, there is only the same fear, hate, and bitterness, with Milton finally attempting to choke Helen and both of them admitting that their lives have ended in "Nothing."

The second double journey in *Lie Down in Darkness* is that of Peyton's journey to her death. In this journey, as in that of Helen and Milton, the present action is a coherent passage through time to a specific goal (Peyton's activities on the day of her death, ending with her suicide), while the past action is Peyton's disordered memory of the passage through life which has brought her to this day. And here, too, the present narrative contains both an element of hope and a deflating "Waste Land" parallel.

Except for a brief opening section in which Harry and his friend Lenny are shown claiming Peyton's body on Hart's Island (New York's potter's field), Peyton's entire double journey is represented through her interior monologue. Styron's model for this abrupt shift to Peyton's consciousness is less Faulkner than Joyce. Both Molly Bloom and Peyton conclude novels in which they have appeared (but have not hitherto been used as centers of perception) with lengthy sections of interior monologue and both of their monologues link, through association, precise description of immediate external detail and fragmentary recollections of the past. Peyton's memory of her life is therefore communicated to us not in the form of lengthy scenes, as are Helen's and Milton's conscious recollections of the past, but through the obsessive symbols and images of her disordered unconscious. Although she tries to suppress her memory of home and family—"I knew I mustn't think of this" (356), she often tells herself—she is hounded by these memories in the shape of their symbolic analogues—the clock, birds, chimes, and drowning images which crowd her mind throughout the day.

Peyton at the opening of her monologue is in pain and misery but she too has hopes for a reconciliation with someone she has loved in the past. Milton had hoped to "cure" Helen and then to be reunited with her; Peyton wishes to find Harry and then convince him that they can live together in peace and harmony, a reunion which she images as their retreat into the interior of a clock. But Harry, when Peyton finds him at the end of the day, cannot be convinced. The clock to him is a clock, and the Peyton he sees before him, though he wishes to help her, is the one who has disillusioned him about love and faithfulness and promises to be "a good girl" (381). So Peyton's hope of escape into a womb-like oblivion of love is lost, and—throwing the clock down a sewer—she turns to the more certain resource of death.

We are prepared for Peyton's failure to persuade Harry by two characteristics of her soliloquy. The first is that the symbols which represent both her illness and the power of the past in her life— birds, chimes, drowning—increase in prominence as the day advances. Initially, they exist only in her memory of past events, but more and more they move into an immediate hallucinatory present in which she feels herself accompanied by birds and threatened by drowning. But also, as in Helen and Milton's journey to the cemetery, the present of Peyton's journey contains an ironic "Waste Land" motif—ironic because the passage through the wasteland of modern life ends not in a potential rebirth but in the confirmation of darkness and death. Hart's Island, which combines a waste disposal plant and a potter's field, is an explicit symbol of the city as wasteland. And Manhattan itself, as Peyton wanders through it in search of Harry, contains a strand of the sexual element in Eliot's wasteland imagery. The animal yet mechanical lower-class sexuality of Tony the milkman and the effete and homosexual upper class world of Albert Berger's Greenwich Village apartment are parallel to Eliot's gramophone and burnished throne sections in "The Waste Land." And finally, after her passage through a world which is the symbolic equivalent of spiritual sterility, Peyton—as she stands naked by the window of the Harlem building—also hears thunder (378, 386). But there is no cleansing or regeneration for Peyton in the tower of her chapel perilous; only death.

The journeys of the Loftises toward Nothing, toward physical and spiritual death, are accompanied by their tortured efforts—as well as the efforts of others—to answer the questions: Why have our lives gone astray, and Who is to blame? Milton and comparable weak figures frequently offer the response that no one is to blame, that life is determined by events beyond the control of an individual. The context of this defense, however, almost always suggests that its function is not to present an authorially sanctioned philosophical statement but to characterize its user as someone who requires excuses for his weakness of will. For example, when Milton is about to begin his affair with Dolly, he thinks, "What had happened had happened and what might happen *would* happen, and so he took a drink and let his knee rest against Dolly's, safe in the all-inclusive logic of determinism" (97). In this instance Styron's irony is blatant. It is less so but still evident later in the novel when the half-drunk Milton defends himself at Peyton's wedding on the old deterministic grounds of man's uncontrollable animal nature. "Maybe we're all just too highstrung," he thinks. "They should have never put the idea of love in the mind of an animal"

(310). But perhaps the most convincing evidence of Styron's belief in the self-serving purpose of the clichés of philosophical determinism is the consoling explanation which Pookie Bonner's vacuous and platitudinous girl friend offers Milton for the mess he has made of his life. " 'A lot of life,' " she tells the drunken Milton at Charlottesville, " 'is governed by circumstances and a lot of these things a person just couldn't help'" (204). It is not surprising, therefore, that as Milton waits at the station dock for the arrival of Peyton's body he takes refuge in the belief that he has not been responsible for her death. Feeling "tricked and defeated" as "a wave of self-pity swept over him," he recalls his father's advice many years ago to fight the temptations of the flesh and replies to the ghost of that counsel, "Not just that, Papa. Other things. Life tends toward a moment [of decision]. Not just the flesh. Not a poet or a thief [that is, lacking a heroic or decisive nature], I could never exercise free will" (14–15). And he goes on to blame his father for spoiling him in his youth and thus contributing to his weakness.

Milton in this instance has adopted a variant form of a conventional deterministic rejection of the possibility of moral responsibility; he does not blame circumstances in general but rather a specific person. As the lives of the Loftises unfold before us, Helen is the one most frequently blamed for their condition, as her hate breeds powerful counter-emotions. To Carey she is at fault because "She would *not* compromise, she would make no concessions" (141), while to Peyton "she was beyond hope . . . the day she was born" (317). And Dolly says of the disturbed Peyton, just before death, that "it's not [Milton's] fault, it's the fault of that succubus who treated her so badly" (76). Milton is also capable of blaming both Helen and Peyton, as when he sees himself as an unwilling catalyst of feminine antagonisms within the triangle. "It had always been he himself," he reflects, "who had been at the focus of these appalling, baffling female emotions. . . . None of his actions, whether right or wrong, had caused this tragedy, so much as the pure fact of himself, his very existence, interposed weaponless and defenseless in a no-man's land between two desperate, warring female machines" (284). Perhaps the most troublesome and muddled attribution of blame to others is Peyton's frequently noted statement, just before she has sex for the first time, that the so-called Lost Generation—the generation of her parents—" 'weren't lost. What they were doing was losing us. . . . They didn't lose themselves, they lost us—you and me'" (235). Here Peyton is not,

I think, speaking for Styron, as has usually been assumed. Helen and Milton have of course contributed to Peyton's flawed nature, just as Milton's father contributed to his weaknesses. But Peyton, like Milton awaiting Peyton's body, is seeking at this moment of moral crisis to shift the responsibility for her actions to a previous generation. She is pursuing not moral precision but psychological relief.

Yet another response to the fate of the Loftises, one with greater authorial sanction, is also to ask who is to blame, since such tragedy demands explanations, but to find no answer. Milton, for example, observes Helen at Peyton's birthday party and senses the profound changes that have occurred in her since their marriage. The beauty and calm of the girl he loved have been replaced by something vicious and destructive. "Where," he asks himself in heartfelt wonder, "did all this rest come from? When?" (94). And in one of the most moving moments of the novel, Harry thinks, as he and Lenny identify Peyton's body in her pauper's grave, *"I just don't know whose fault it is"* (334).

In this reflection by Harry—the one (and almost fulsomely) "positive" character in the novel—we come close to Styron's sense of the dilemma of moral judgment and responsibility posed by the tragedy of the Loftises. In a 1965 interview Styron was asked for his views on free will and determinism and specifically if Peyton was "in a sense determined." He replied,

> That's the old question, isn't it? Hopefully not unanswerable. . . . Yes, I think everybody has free will. I think that events tend to alter our free will; certain tragic events or certain aspects of a man's nature can tend to sort of warp and twist his will, so that it becomes a conditional free will.[14]

And when asked whether he thought Helen was not "an almost totally evil woman," he replied,

> You're right. I think I was trying to portray a woman who was irredeemably ugly, by nature. They exist. And maybe it's an unanswerable question whether it's the product of the wicked series of events; it's too infinitely complex to claim that there's an answer to it. . . . The morality is so complex that it's almost unamenable to discussion.[15]

Styron, in this interview and in *Lie Down in Darkness*, wishes to suggest both the terrible power of circumstances to condition free will and the human desire, usually tragic in outcome, to know and to resist this power. The interaction of free will and circumstances in the past, and the desire in the present to fathom this interaction as it occurred in the past and as it impinges on the present, make for the complexity of life—and of fiction which seeks to represent this aspect of experience. *Lie Down in Darkness* is not a novel which provides answers; it rather engages us in the torment of those who seek answers but cannot find satisfactory ones.

It is this effect of complexity dramatized but "unamenable" to analysis which Styron attempts to convey in a number of different ways in the novel. So, for example, after the first extended depiction of a Loftis family disaster, the Sunday lawn gathering, Styron himself comments that all the participants in the event were "perhaps conscious of a clean spring twilight laden with cedar and the smell of the sea, and of something else, also: the cluster around them of quiet, middle-class homes, hedged and pruned and proper, all touched at this moment by a somber trouble; while each mind, too, perhaps turned inward for an instant, like the soul that forever seeks a grave, upon his own particular guilt" (63). It is this motif of indistinguishably shared guilt which Carey Carr picks up and endorses after Peyton's death: "Who, finally, lest it be God himself, could know where the circle, composed as it was of such tragic suspicions and misunderstandings, began, and where it ended? Who was the author of the original misdeed?" (239).

Thus, though many characters in *Lie Down in Darkness* search for someone or something to blame, the effect of the novel is not of specific responsibility but of life as conditioned by the interwoven dynamics of existence, as shaped by the textures of our personalities and worlds in so impenetrable yet powerful a fashion that we are both dumbfounded by our lack of control while still seeking to maintain control. For this effect, as in almost all other phases of the novel, the journey structure is of paramount importance. The principal impact of a novel set only superficially in the present and devoted almost entirely to the psychological and emotional wounds of the past is to enforce on us the conditioned nature of our lives. Milton may hope to "cure" Helen, and Peyton may hope to win back Harry, but because we know in full dramatic detail what Milton, Helen, and Peyton have been we also know how impossible are their hopes—that the patterns of response shaped by their lives are irreversible, that their wounds will never heal. We also feel how futile is their effort to be free of the past because this desire requires a reversal of the flow of time and a return to the start of their journeys—to childhood innocence for Peyton and to early love for Milton and Helen—while these journeys are in fact characterized by the increasingly destructive emotions of adulthood. The train which leaves Port Warwick departs—in the final words of the novel—into "oncoming night" (400) rather than the new dawn hoped for by the Loftises. *Lie Down in Darkness* leaves us not with an effect of simplistic determinism but rather with a sense that the formulaic clichés of naturalism have been denied in favor of a more profound and complex naturalistic vision of the conditioned nature of experience. "The agony of human error" in *Lie Down in Darkness*, Frederick Hoffman remarks, "is so great that there is no real center of blame."[16] There is instead a center of naturalistic tragic compassion.

Saul Bellow

The Adventures of Augie March

Saul Bellow's third novel, published in 1953 when he was thirty-eight, differs sharply from his first two works of fiction, *Dangling Man* (1944) and *The Victim* (1947). These are novels of conscious compression and chill intellectuality in which the theme of man as victim and sufferer predominates.[1] In *The Adventures of Augie March*, however, Bellow sought a new manner and a new theme, as is suggested by his choice of a picaresque title. Informality, looseness, and a corresponding expansiveness of subject matter characterize this new work. The book "came easily," Bellow later recalled. "I kicked over the traces, wrote catch-as-catch-can, picaresque. I took my chance."[2] This "chance" included Bellow's endowing Augie with one of the most richly evocative prose styles in modern American fiction, a style dense with colloquial diction and rhythms (often Yiddish in origin), with classical, literary, and historical allusions, and with frequent echoes of Thoreau, Whitman, and Mark Twain. They also include his creation of Augie as an urban Jewish transcendental hero—a figure Chicago-born but seeking his identity and thus his fate with confidence that at the center of his nature (the "axial lines" of self) there lie as well the great moral absolutes of life: truth, love, peace, and harmony.

Augie March has therefore often been viewed as Bellow's most engaging novel but as both simpler and more positive than either his earlier or later fiction. The appeal of the work, it is felt, lies largely in its "gritty social texture"[3] (particularly the depiction of Augie's Chicago youth) and in the witty freedom of Augie's narrative style. Augie's quest for a "better fate" is an appropriately self-apparent theme within this obviousness and looseness of form and style. In fact, however, *The Adventures of Augie March* is neither ingenuous nor obvious. Rather it explores with considerable complexity and depth the naturalistic absorption in the precarious balance between the conditioning forces of life and man's desire and need to discover centers of value and affirmation despite the presence of these forces.[4]

Perhaps the best way to introduce this theme is not through such often cited passages as the breezy opening or the "axial lines" section or the Columbus metaphor of the final lines but rather in the incident of Augie and the maid Jacqueline in the last chapter of the novel. Augie is dropping off the old, fat, and ugly Jacqueline at her Normandy home for Christmas when their car breaks down and they have to trudge the last few miles through the mud. Jacqueline tells him, as they sing to keep warm, of her dream of going to Mexico some day, a dream which Augie later recalls as he continues his journey to Bruges on a cold and dark December afternoon, amid the ruins of war.

> But, thinking of Jacqueline and Mexico, I got to grinning again. That's the *animal ridens* in me, the laughing creature, forever rising up. What's so laughable, that a Jacqueline, for instance, as hard used as that by rough forces, will still refuse to lead a disappointed life? Or is the laugh at nature—including eternity—that it thinks it can win over us and the power of hope? Nah, nah! I think. It never will. But that probably is the joke, on one or the other, and laughing is an enigma that includes both.[5]

Augie March is about the "rough forces" of experience, about all that compels and conditions and shapes man, particularly the shaping power of other human wills. It is also about the darkness in nature, the nature of decay and death rather than of eternal renewal. And it is also about the human effort to maintain hope despite these realities, the hope which musters as much grace and wit as is possible in the face of the permanent and insoluble enigma of man's condition. *Augie March*, in short, for all its comic vibrancy, picaresque swiftness of movement, and larky prose is also a naturalistic novel of ideas. Events and people represent specific phases of Augie's effort to understand both the "rough forces" of life and the nature of hope. They represent as well specific contributions to his ultimate discovery that in comic awareness there is a means toward accommodation, if not resolution, of the fundamental conflict between experience and expectation.

Bellow has often commented in his interviews and essays that "we live among ideas"[6] and that "it is a great defect of American novelists that they shun thinking."[7] But Bellow the ideologue—the honor graduate in anthropology and the *Encyclopedia Brittanica* editor—is also Bellow the admirer of "hard facts"[8] in fiction who was first drawn to the possibilities of the novel by his interest in the midwest realists.[9] These two qualities of Bellow the novelist merge in *The Adventures of Augie March* to produce a picaresque novel in which Augie's adventures are not only among ideas but themselves represent a number of large-scale ideas. Augie is both a Chicago-bred youth of the 1920s and 30s and the universal seeker of the permanent values of life. He is a grail quester in the guise of a young man from the city, and the grail he seeks is his own identity.

One of Augie's major characteristics as a seeker is his pretense of dullness or ignorance—somewhat like Henry James' Maisie or Mark Twain's Huck Finn—in order to avoid capture by the armed marauders of the world. He is also—and more significantly—like Dreiser's Carrie in that his seemingly aimless drifting, which includes a willingness to be convinced and directed, is in fact a capacity to drift in directions which he himself desires. Augie for the most part is an absorber and receiver, "a listener by upbringing," who gives "soft answers" to affronts (72, 81). Part of his survival capacity derives from his ability to absorb the hard knocks of experience without "special grief, . . . being by and large too larky and boisterous" to take them "to heart" (12). To survive while continuing to search, without doing harm to others, is his operative ethic; all other moral questions are a matter of context. He steals on several occasions but not on others, despite the opportunity, and he sleeps with some girls but not with one who appears reluctant, since "you never know what forms self-respect will take" (243). As the archetypal seeker, he is above all, despite occasional dry thoughts in dry seasons, a man of hope. After the disappointments and calamities of his Mexican adventure, he is "aged by hard going and experience" (431) and "more larky formerly than now" (447), but the close of the novel still finds him a believer in "the power of hope" (536).

Augie's world also has an unchanging character despite his twenty years of adventure in Chicago, Mexico, New York, and Europe. Because Augie is everywhere a seeker of his own identity, he finds everywhere those anxious for various suspect reasons to offer themselves as guides. Only the superficial character of life changes—

man as Machiavelli, as manipulator of others for his own ends, is omnipresent.[10] Bellow expresses this theme of the repetitive nature of experience in a number of ways. One is the device usually foreign to the picaresque novel of the reappearing and unchanging minor character. Augie back in Chicago after his Mexican venture soon encounters almost all the figures, in their accustomed "humour" roles, who made up his Chicago experience before his journey, and several of these characters later reappear in New York and Paris. It is perhaps above all Sylvester, a drifter like Augie whom Augie meets some half-dozen or more times in wildly unlikely places, who symbolizes the notion that Augie's world is the same wherever he goes. It is no wonder that at the close of the novel, even while living in Paris, Augie can claim that "it's all the same to me where I live" (531). Another way in which Bellow enforces the theme of the unity of experience is by enclosing Augie's adventures within a repetitive mesh of personal relationships, in which someone always knows someone else—not only in Chicago, where the device is almost a running joke—but elsewhere as well. So, for example, in an incident which epitomizes this aspect of the novel, Augie in a lifeboat in the North Atlantic finds that he and the only other occupant of the boat are from the same Chicago neighborhood and have acquaintances in common.

Perhaps the most striking evidence of Bellow's insistence on the underlying similarity of all experience is his attitude toward the past. Of course, he suggests in *Augie March* that the distant past and the present are different in many superficial ways, and that they are significantly different in that the values derived from a pastoral world have little meaning in a modern urban civilization. But at the heart of Augie's adventures is the assumption that the figures he encounters—figures who constitute his experience of the present—are universal types with evocative historical proto-types. As a reader of the Harvard Classics, among other such works, Augie is aware of these parallels and thus often creates a rich layer of allusion to suggest the similarities between past and present. This is a strategy we are most familiar with in modern literature in the "epic" poetry of Eliot and Pound. Augie adopts this technique, however, not to suggest the decay of value in the present, which is Eliot and Pound's intent, but rather, as in his comparison of Einhorn to Ceasar, Ulysses, and Louis XIV (or as in Bellow's own "Roman texture" in the novel as a whole, with such character names as Augustus, Thea, Stella, and Caligula) to suggest the permanence and continuity of the heroic temperament, even in a crippled Chicago small-time operator. When Einhorn also indulges in such comparisons, Augie comments, "If you want to pick your own ideal creature in the mirror coastal air and sharp leaves of ancient perfections and be at home where a great mankind was at home, I've never seen any reason why not" (76).

Yet the theme of the unchanging in time and place—and therefore of the archetypal in Augie's quest—is but one of two major threads in *Augie March*. For within the broad configuration of the statically universal in Augie's experience is also a theme of variation and change. Augie encounters different kinds of pressure to accept some qualification of his quest, and he gradually clarifies the nature of his search. The naturalism of *Augie March* lies in the collision at various points in the novel of experience and vision.

"Experience"—for Augie, his "adventures"—is principally social, and "vision" also arises from an understanding of oneself in relation to others. Augie rejects the two traditional alternative sources of wisdom—the plumbing of nature and the isolation of the self. The modern world, he soon discovers, contains "no shepherd-Sicily, no free-hand nature-painting" where he can find his Edenic self, but only "deep city vexations" where "you are forced early into deep city aims" (84). Complete withdrawal into the self is also dismissed by Augie. His friend, the "melancholy and brilliant" Kayo Obermark, "thought the greatest purity was outside human relations, that those only begot lies and cabbage-familiarity" (259). But though Augie admires the intellectual idealism of Kayo's view, he also resists it. "I had the idea," he thinks, "that you don't take so wide a stand that it makes a human life impossible, nor try to bring together irreconcilables that destroy you, but try out what of human you can live with first." "Imperfection," Augie concludes, "is always the condition as found; all great beauty too, my scratched eyeballs will always see scratched" (260).

So when Augie early in the novel offers the Whitmanesque formula that "all the influences were lined up waiting for me. I was born, and there they were to form me, which is why I tell you more of them than of myself" (13), he means people, just as at the end of the novel he means people when he remarks that he will continue his quest among "those near-at-hand" (536). The people in Augie's life have a general sameness, as I noted earlier and as Tony Tanner states even more strongly in his comment that they "tend to add up to a sort of general presence of the not-Augie as opposed to the Augie."[11] The "not-Augie" figures in Augie's life do indeed share a number of qualities. Many of them are like the owner of a dog grooming service for whom Augie works briefly. The owner's relations with the animals, Augie recalls, "was a struggle. He was trying to wrest something from them. I don't know what. Perhaps that their conception of a dog should be what his was" (185). Figures of this kind wish to help Augie, to groom him for life (in fact, many do reclothe him), but they also wish him to share their conception of what he is. "Sharing" is thus a loaded term in *Augie March*: it implies the use of someone for one's own emotional or psychological purposes disguised as a wish to help. As Augie says of a particularly troublesome friend in Mexico, "He saw to it that his lot was shared, like everybody else, and did something with you to compel you to feel what he felt" (368). Augie's relations with such figures are similar to that of Huck Finn with the Duke and Dauphin. Augie resists them as best he can, but he is saved largely by the inherent weakness of the figures—Grandma Lausch's pride, Thea's inhumanity, Basteshaw's "brain fever"—which causes their fall from power. Yet Augie, like Huck, often finds himself pitying and looking after those who sought to control him and mold his fate.

Not all of the "not-Augie" characters in *Augie March* are Machiavellian controllers. The influences which are lined up in wait for Augie include several different kinds of relationship, from the crudest users of raw power in order to control to those who shape and mold through the giving of themselves in love. The reappearance of basically similar types in Augie's life suggests that the form of *Augie March* is only superficially the linear one of most picaresque fiction, in which different kinds of adventures follow each other in no apparent order. *Augie March* is really a series of circles, of repetitive patterns without end as Augie encounters again and again characters whose involvement with him represents a reappearance of one of the basic ways in which one person affects another. *Augie March* is therefore much like *U.S.A.* in that the superficially disparate—the twelve narratives of *U.S.A.*, the many adventures of Augie—in fact constitute a deeply interwoven and thematically unified structure.

The earliest cluster of figures whom Augie encounters is that of a number of "adopters"—those who in the act of helping Augie as a fatherless and almost destitute youth also require that he play specific roles within their families. Grandma Lausch is the first such figure in Augie's life. Deprived of a base in her own family because her daughters-in-law refuse to countenance her domineering ways, she "adopts" all the Marches in order to fulfill her need "to direct a house, to command, to govern, to manage, scheme, devise, and intrigue" (5). Her shrewdness and strength of will contribute to the survival of the Marches, but she asks in return obedience and fear. Her hold is broken when she as well as Augie and his brother Simon grow older, and Augie next comes under the influence of the Coblins, an earthy and generous family for whom he works. Since the Coblins have a son who has run away to the marines and a daughter who stutters, they welcome Augie as a candidate for both son and son-in-law. But though Augie is attracted by the larger-than-life warmth and vitality of the Coblins, he resists these roles and moves on to the Renlings. The Renlings are well-to-do—they clothe Augie in princely fashion from their store—and thus offer him a major social advance. But Mrs. Renling is childless and wishes to enclose Augie in the silken threads of her maternal longing. When she mentions adoption, Augie flees her "tender weights" (152). The last and most powerful of the families which want to adopt Augie are the Magnuses. Large, gross, vulgar, and extremely rich, they have already absorbed and almost devoured Simon, providing him with both a wife and a business. They offer to Augie the luxury and power of great wealth, of an opulence which intimates that he is to be adopted not so much by the family as by "things themselves" (238).

From Grandma Lausch to the Magnuses, the "adopters" derive their strength from Augie's material needs. As Augie matures, however, he comes under the equally powerful influence of "true believers" who seek to enlist him in the pursuit of their vision of life. These are the "theoreticians" whom Augie berates toward the close of the novel—the "big personalities, destiny molders, and heavy-water brains, Machiavellis and wizard evildoers, big-wheels and imposers-upon, absolutists" (524). The appeal of these figures is analogous to that of the adopters. The first offer the security of material comfort, the second of unquestioning belief. The first provide within the closed structure of the family a refuge against the world, the second within the equally closed structures of such intellectual systems as primitivism and scientism an equally snug refuge against intrusive ideas. Yet both in fact are prisons of body, mind, and spirit.

Thea is Augie's first major theoretician. Augie is drawn to her initially by her extraordinary will and "strong nerve" (145) and then is bound by his love. He accompanies her to Mexico because "I went where and as she said and did whatever she wanted because I was threaded to her as if through the skin" (315). Her goal in Mexico is ostensibly to train an eagle in falconry, but in reality it is to uncover in animal life the courage and strength of will which she believes lacking in man and, more specifically, in Augie. If Caligula the eagle can be trained to display these qualities, perhaps Augie can; perhaps man, in short, can rise to the purity of animal power. But in a wonderfully comic parody of the primitivism of Lawrence's *The Plumed Serpent* and Hemingway's *Death in the Afternoon* and *The Green Hills of Africa*, Caligula turns out to be not a "cruel machine" of nature but cautious and even cowardly (355).[12] His fear of the sharp-clawed lizards which he is asked to hunt confirms not the potential inhumanity of man but the potential humanity of animals. As Augie wryly comments after one of Caligula's failures, "Well, it was hard to take this from wild nature, that there should be humanity mixed with it" (355). Man, with his "faulty humanity" (379), cannot absorb from nature codes of life which in fact do not exist either in man or in nature. Thea the theoretician cannot accept this, and she responds to Caligula's failure by discarding both him and Augie and by moving on to snakes. "'You're not special,'" she tells Augie. "'You're like everybody else'" (396).

The other major theoretician whom Augie encounters is Basteshaw, the biologist and ship's carpenter with whom he shares a lifeboat after their freighter is torpedoed during the war. If Thea wishes to confirm an idea about nature, Basteshaw wishes in his experiments to manipulate nature itself. Neither has respect for nature or man, only for the imperatives of his own belief. Basteshaw wants to discover the secret of the origin of life, and when Augie resists enlistment in this effort ("Damn you guys," he cries, "you don't care how you fiddle with nature" [506]), he finds himself batted over the head with an oar and made part of it willy-nilly. So the mad scientists of the world, Bellow's miniature allegory goes, have made us all captives of their "fiddling" with nature.[13]

The adopters and theoreticians in Augie's life wish to control him. But Augie also encounters two other important groups of figures in his adventures who, though they occasionally use him, function principally to reveal to him the nature and dangers of the pursuit of an independent fate. The first such group consists of characters who appear to be seeking their own destinies but who in fact are fulfilling themselves only superficially or incompletely. Sylvester is an obvious example of a figure of this kind. Trying this and that—movie manager, engineer, subway guard, revolutionary—in all parts of the world, he appears to mirror Augie's own life. But unlike Augie, his "adventures" are without a center; he is merely physically footloose and intellectually unanchored and he thus reveals that to move is not necessarily to seek.[14]

Augie's brother Simon is a far more significant foil to Augie's quest. Of Augie's two brothers, Georgie is mentally defective and therefore "simple" while Simon is shrewd and worldly. He appears to be pursuing his fate with insight and strength as with "singleness of purpose" (29) he seeks to reach particular goals at particular moments of his life—to be top boy in high school, to be a gentleman, and to have attractive women and great wealth. He is a kind of latter-day Frank Cowperwood (who also flourished in the tough competitive world of Chicago) in that he too makes "I satisfy myself" the guiding principle of his life. " 'You don't care what happens to anybody else as long as you get yours' " (196), he tells Augie. He gets his by becoming a Magnus and thus acquiring Cadillacs and mistresses. But if Augie is in part Simon in his fondness for opulence, Simon is in part Augie in that he cannot be happy in an identity which is not entirely his own. " 'We're the same and want the same' " (199), he tells Augie, meaning that they both desire the power of wealth. But their more important similarity is that neither is comfortable playing roles. Simon therefore desperately hopes that Augie will also marry into the Magnus family and thus confirm the role of loud vulgarian which is now Simon's as a Magnus. The violent rage with which Simon confronts all life by the end of the novel is really a rage against himself. If Sylvester's mobility is directionless, Simon's success is empty. In the end, he is simple Simon.

Whereas the fates of Sylvester and Simon suggest to Augie that in the pursuit of one's identity the means can be confused with the end, Einhorn and Mintouchian express values which help Augie in the crystallization of the nature of his quest. They are, in short, less foils than mentors, albeit themselves flawed examples of the values they endorse.

Einhorn, whom Augie meets while still in early adolescence, remains for him throughout the novel a source of admiration for his "philosophical capacity" (60) and his freedom from custom and cant. Augie particularly values Einhorn's desire to be free from the ideological bonds which tie most men. "'There's law, and then there's Nature,'" he tells Augie. "'There's opinion and then there's Nature. Somebody has to get outside of law and opinion and speak for Nature'" (67). So Einhorn is "absolutely outspoken about vital things" (74). As Augie remarks, "Much that was nameless to many people through disgust or shame he didn't mind naming to himself or to a full confidant (or pretty nearly so) like me, and caught, used, and worked all feelings freely" (68). The deep irony of Einhorn's life is that he himself is severely crippled and is thus seemingly a victim of the nature he speaks for. But the same spirit which refuses to accept convention will not accept that desire can be confined and limited by a wheelchair. As far as sex is concerned, "He wouldn't stay a cripple, Einhorn; he couldn't hold his soul in it" (78).

Augie comes to esteem Einhorn greatly—particularly for "the fight he had made on his sickness" (100)—and to recognize the complexity and richness of his character beneath the layer of petty shystering. Einhorn is thus something of a naturalistic hero—a figure of depth and pathos despite his shabby ways. In one of the more striking scenes of the novel, we encounter him taking Augie to a whorehouse as a high school graduation present and riding on Augie's back from the car to the house composed and dignified, with aplomb and in control. He is also something of a father to Augie and is well positioned to effect an "adoption," since he offers both an understanding of Augie's character ("'You've got *opposition* in you'" [117]) and an illustration of the ideal of freedom. Yet Augie holds back because he senses an important limitation in Einhorn's character—that he does not understand the nature of love. For out of his needs and out of his philosophical materialism, Einhorn conceives of relations between the sexes as entirely physical and of relations among men as destructively competitive. He cannot understand, for example, Augie's unwillingness to revenge himself on Simon (who has wronged Augie and deserves vengeance) because Augie loves Simon, since he holds that "in the naked form of the human jelly, one should choose or seize with force" (183). So Augie drifts away from Einhorn, despite what he has learned from him. He senses that his fate is neither the role nor the burden of the youth who bore Einhorn to the whorehouse.

Late in the novel, Augie meets Mintouchian, a figure who closely resembles Einhorn, as Augie himself remarks. An operator on an morning. They can't change. So maybe you're lucky. But others are stuck; they have what they have; and if that's their truth, where are we?" (254–55) But, Augie responds, "Me, I couldn't think all was so poured in concrete and that there weren't occasions for happiness that weren't illusions of people still permitted to be forgetful of permanent disappointment, more or less permanent pain . . ; and maybe most intolerable the hardening of detestable character, like bone" (255). Augie himself lives out these qualifications [of a] conditioned life. He escapes a slum fate in part because of his [know]wledge of that fate, and he and Mimi find that all is not poured [c]oncrete, that happiness can be real despite the deep disap[point]ments of life caused by permanent flaws of character. Mimi [beco]mes pregnant by the aloof and self-centered political science [studen]t Hooker Frazer and requires an abortion. But unlike Rob[erta,] *An American Tragedy*, whose pregnancy is an example of the [ ] of human powerlessness, she and Augie discover, in the [ef]fort to resolve her dilemma, "occasional happiness"— [happ]iness of their pride and strength of will and mutual com[ ] as they work together, in the face of the indifference and [o]f their Chicago boarding house world, to liberate her [c]ondition.

[Mexi]co, Augie feels himself especially powerless, caught as [by his] love for Thea. Nevertheless, in a moment of insight he [gains a] deep understanding of the compensations for power[lessness wi]thin the human condition. On a porch he notices some [flowers, a]nd also a small caged animal, and comments: "It said [ ]hat these flowers should have no power over their [appe]arance, nor over the time, and yet be such a success [and] plaster the insignificant wall. I saw also the little [animal] roved over his square of cage in every dimension, [ ]ackwards. In the depth of accident, you be sup[pl]y but at sleeping time" (366).[16] The rebellious and [s]elf-preserving knowledge, occasional happiness, [ ]eness—so we not only endure but often flourish [condit]ioned existence, in our cages of whatever kind. [Comper]nsations, Augie claims, exist not merely in our [h]opes (the conventional source of compensation) [wor]ld," as Augie himself has found during his ad[venture] tries to create a world he can live in, and what [ ] can't see. But the real world is already cre[ated and if our fab]rication doesn't correspond, then even if you

international scale, as Einhorn was in the Chicago neighborhoods, Mintouchian, like Einhorn, recognizes few restraints to his personal freedom while expressing an appealing philosophical position. "A great man," Augie comments, "he was another of those persons who persistently arise before me with life counsels and illuminations" (478). Appropriately as an internationalist of the 1940s, Mintouchian's principal "illumination" is an existential emphasis on man's need for self-definition through experience. He tells Augie, who requires endorsement of this idea at this point, " 'You must take your chance on what you are. And you can't sit still. . . . It is better to die what you are than to live a stranger forever' " (485). But again like Einhorn, Mintouchian is flawed in his distrust of love. Since he believes that all life, including love, is change, he is unable to accept that love can exist without the deception and deceit which change brings. For Augie, who is about to marry Stella, this view is as unacceptable as was Einhorn's advice about Simon.

———————

Augie's journey through life in search of his identity involves not only encounters with those who are able to influence his sense of himself—the adopters, theoreticians, and counselors of the world— but also experience of the permanent and irremediable conditions of life which threaten selfhood itself. The most important of these conditions is that of the inevitability of material dissolution and thus the certainty that death and oblivion are the only ends we can know. Augie's quest contains the fundamental irony that the process of finding oneself in time is also that of losing oneself. No wonder that he responds feelingly to Einhorn's fear of death, "who maybe was the only real god he had" (83), and that he remarks that "it takes some of us a long time to find out what the price is of being in nature, and what the facts are about your tenure" (362). In Mexico, where graves and corpses are neglected, Augie observes "how openly death is received everywhere, in the beauty of the place, and how it is acknowledged that anyone may be roughly handled—the proudest—pinched, slapped, and set down, thrown down; for death throws even worse in men's faces and makes it horrible and absurd that one never touched should be roughly dumped under, dumped upon" (338). And the meaning of this unavoidable reality, Augie comes to recognize fully at the close of the novel in a Europe crowded with ancient and fresh dead, is that

"Death is going to take the boundaries away from us, that we should no more be persons. That's what death is about" (519).

Death in its "rough handling" of human individuality has an equivalent in life itself—the "darkness" of man at his most indiscriminately bestial and thus least distinctive and individual. In a West Side police station, in a strikingly Dreiserian passage, Augie notes that

> it was very dark. It was spoiled, diseased, sore and running. And as the mis-minted and wrong-struck figures and faces stooped, shambled, strode, gazed, dreaded, surrendered, didn't care—unfailing, the surplus and superabundance of human material—you wondered that all was stuff that was born human and shaped human, and over the indiscriminateness and lack of choice. (229)

Yet despite the "rough handling" of death and the "darkness" of animal man (images which are to peak in Augie's final reflections about Jacqueline), man, Augie decides, still must live and hope. After his criminal friend Joe Gorman—a figure out of *Studs Lonigan*—is captured and beaten by the police, a depressed Augie makes his way back to Chicago:

> However, as I felt on entering Erie, Pennsylvania, there is a darkness. It is for everyone. . . . Only some Greeks and admirers of theirs, in their liquid noon, where the friendship of beauty to human things was perfect, thought they were clearly divided from this darkness. And these Greeks too were in it. But still they are the admiration of the rest of the mud-sprung, famine-knifed, street pounding, war-rattled, painstaking, kicked in the belly, grief and cartilage mankind. (175)

We accept that darkness is for everybody, but we admire those who believe in the light, and we model our lives on this paradox. So Augie decides to write up his "adventures" not because this act will help him to escape oblivion but as an act of "being what he is" and thus of living in the spirit of Greek (and existential) idealism. He writes, he tells us, "not in order to be so highly significant but probably because human beings have the power to say and ought to employ it at the proper time. When finally you're done speaking

you're dumb forever after, and when you're through s—
go still, but this is no reason to decline to speak and —
what you are" (519).

Bellow wrote in a characteristic statement in 196—
ciety with its titanic products conditions but canno—
nature us. It forces certain elements of the genius —
go into hiding."[15] Augie's adventures occur wi—
since they are experiences which identify the —
of modern life while revealing the difficulty —
humanity and selfhood. Because Augie's ider—
can express it only in opposition (his "grea—
tance and to say No!" [117]) or in vaguenes—
[28]). "What did I . . . want for myself?"—
couldn't have told you. . . . I knew I long—
understand for what" (84). So Augie "tr—
throughout his career—from the intel—
ing, from the coal business to the int—
at the close of the novel is still do—
pilgrimage of mine" (424). He do—
not to make up my mind and be—
As he tells Mintouchian, thoug—
what I am . . ., what if what I —
(485). Augie's aimlessness thu—
To be "in opposition" requi—
seeking control are everywh—
is so much in doubt.

Throughout his indefi—
counters the view that —
them. Einhorn suppor—
perience when he n—
large number of cri—
mined,'" he says. B—
ideas when he tel—
mined for you to—
tioning force, —
force. Later, —
more signific—
ism—that o—
effect of ou—
that most —
are, such—

feel noble and insist on there being something better than what people call reality, that better something needn't try to exceed what, in its actuality, since we know it so little, may be very surprising" (378).

Augie's "axial lines of life" declaration is thus not an isolated triumphant discovery of man's distinctive potential (as it is often viewed) but rather one of a number of compensations for man's conditioned state which Augie has found. Augie, as he tells his friend Clem, "was lying on the couch here before and they [the axial lines] went quivering right straight through me. Truth, love, peace, bounty, usefulness, harmony!'" (454) This experience of truth, Augie realizes, is available to all men, to "'man himself, finite and taped as he is. . . . Even his pains will be joy if they are true, even his helplessness will not take away his power. . . . The embrace of other true people will take away his dread of fast change and short life'" (455). Man's helplessness, his condition of finiteness as a "taped" creature within "fast change"—all the rough forces and darkness of life—are not denied in this passage. Rather, they exist in conjunction with various compensating counter forces, in this instance that of the joy and power and community contained in the recognition of the great truths of human aspiration.

It is in the human capacity to love deeply that Bellow in *Augie March* offers his most moving example of the naturalistic paradox which runs throughout the novel—that in imprisonment we still find value and meaning. Augie is first introduced to the idea that love can be a destructive controlling force by Grandma Lausch, who tells him that "'The more you love people the more they'll mix you up'" (9) and by Jimmy Klein, who explains to him that the desire for sex leads inevitably to the prison of the family. But Augie's first major encounter with the full ambivalence of love is in the example of Mimi, whom he meets before he himself falls deeply in love with Thea. Mimi is a hard, tough, spirited girl who is very much like Augie himself in her larkiness and opposition. But she is also a slave to love; all meaning in life for her "rested on the gentleness in privacy of man and woman" (270). Mimi in love is therefore a striking example of the human tendency to engage others in one's own fate—"that everyone sees to it his fate is shared. Or tries to see to it" (211). Mimi's fate is her need to love, and she seeks to enlist others in the fulfillment of this need, with her "recruiting place" her "actual body" and her weapons of persuasion "her clinching will, her hard reason, and her obstinate voice" (211). And although Mimi's need locks her into a deeply troublesome relationship with the distant and neglectful Hooker Frazer, it also brings her a "tough happiness" (253), a sense of fulfillment within pain and enclosure.

So when Augie falls in love with Thea, he knows that he is surrendering a large part of himself in particular his freedom to pursue his own fate—tor love. He realizes that he is "abandoning some mighty old protections which now stood empty. . . . Oh, you chump and weak fool, you are one of a humanity that can't be numbered and not more than the dust of metals scattered in a magnetic field and clinging to the lines of force, determined by laws, eating, sleeping, employed, conveyed, obedient, and subject. So why hunt for still more ways to lose liberty?" (316) Yet Augie, when deeply in love, also believes that love is not only an adequate substitute for an independent fate but that fate itself. He tries to tell Thea that "I had looked all my life for the right thing to do, for a fate good enough, that I had opposed people in what they wanted to make of me, but now that I was in love with her I understood much better what I myself wanted" (318). For Thea, however, as Augie discovers, love is not a value or goal in itself but is rather a means of making Augie into what she wants him to be. No wonder, then, that Augie can later sum up his love experiences as an insoluble paradox: "I didn't want to be what they made of me but wanted to please them. Kindly explain! An independent fate, and love too—what confusion" (401).

Yet Augie ultimately grasps and endorses this paradox despite its contradictions and confusions. Love, he comes to feel, is both a hindrance to an independent fate and a vehicle for the achievement of this goal. Back in Chicago after his Mexican adventure, Augie in a "dry" season expresses to Kayo Obermark his belief that man is shaped by "the technical achievements which try to make you exist in their way" (450). Kayo responds, "What you are talking about is *moha*—a Navajo word, and also Sanskrit, meaning opposition of the finite. It is the Bronx cheer of the conditioning forces. Love is the only answer to *moha*, being infinite. I mean all forms of love, eros, agape, libido, philia, and ecstasy. They are always the same but sometimes one quality dominates and sometimes another" (450).

Augie later believes that his love for Stella confirms Kayo's explanation of the role of love. Not only does Augie feel that he and

Stella are united in opposition since they are "the kind of people other people are always trying to fit into their schemes" (384), but that his love for Stella will permit him to escape the determining forces of life. Or, to use his own imagery, through love he will avoid being a volitionless metal filing sited on a magnetic line but will rather locate himself freely on his own axial lines of meaning. As he explains when he is about to marry Stella, other people "were subject to all the laws in the book, like the mountain peaks leaning toward their respective magnetic poles, or like crabs in the weeds or crystals in the caves. Whereas I, with the help of love, had gotten in on a much better thing and was giving this account of myself that reality comes from and was not just at the mercy" (488).

But of course both Kayo and Augie are in part wrong. Despite the "answer" of love to *moha*, Augie's activities as a black market dealer at the close of the novel contribute to the control of man by his technology. And his relations with Stella return him to the subjugation of love. "I understood," he comments, "that I would mostly do as she wanted because it was I who loved her most" (515). Yet despite Augie's discovery that life has not changed very much since his boyhood in Chicago—that adopters and controllers are still everywhere, and that the rough forces and darkness still flourish—he has himself become a theoretician, a "fanatic" (522), of love, and is willing to take his stand within its ambivalences. For love, he now realizes, in its fusion of the determined and the free, the destructive and the life-enhancing, the other and the self, epitomizes the experience within which man must live and die. Augie at the conclusion of the novel has therefore not ended his adventures. He refuses to lead the disappointed life, despite his disappointments, and will continue to search for his better fate within love of "those near-at-hand" (536)—Stella, a home and children, teaching the young ("It wasn't so much education as love. That was the idea" [514–15]). His quest for meaning and value in that which controls him is not fatuous. It is rather a deeply felt response to the human condition as that condition is perceived within the naturalistic tradition.

Postscript

A major flaw in most discussions of naturalism is the belief that the movement is something new in Western history. Never before, it seems, had man's irrationality and bestiality, his circumscribed will, and his limited understanding been the subject of a serious and major literature. Prostitutes and depraved workmen, animalistic farmers and crazed artists (to note but a few of Zola's major characters) had no doubt appeared in literature before, but they had never been the principal figures of a significant literary movement. Surely, therefore, there was something new under the sun, and this something new undoubtedly derived from and was similar to the materialistic bias of modern science and contemporary society. But to view naturalism in this way is to mistake the surface for the essential. For if one adopts a broad and expansive view of man's conception of himself from the beginning to the present, one realizes that there have always been periods when theologians, philosophers, statesmen, and artists—that is, men attempting to interpret life—have had a bleak estimate of human nature and experience. Often belief during a period of this kind—the belief, say, of a St. Augustine, a Calvin, or a Hobbes—derives from a reaction against an exalted notion of man held during a previous period and a responsiveness to the oppressive conditions of contemporary life. Often this belief thus stresses that man's ability to choose, to express his will consciously and freely, is limited both by his own nature and by the world in which he lives. But this stress, which in every age in which it occurs takes on the distinctive texture and color of that age's social life and intellectual preoccupations, this stress does not preclude the presence of a strain of humanistic value, a strain which also assumes a shape related to the interests and nature of the period. I am, of course, simplifying one of the most profound and complex rhythms in Western thought. But I nevertheless think that it can be granted that man has wavered between extremes of belief throughout history and that these extremes are therefore less absolute commentaries upon human nature and experience than metaphors in a huge and endless historical poem in which the poetic mood wavers continually from doubt and skepticism to celebration and faith.

Naturalism, as a world-wide late nineteenth- and early twentieth-century movement, is one such moment in this poem. And American naturalism, as a specific phase of this world-wide movement, has had its own internal rhythm. Naturalism in America has largely been the product of the response of writers during specific historical moments to the pull both of permanent features of naturalistic expression and of particular naturalistic absorptions of the period. The presence of an internal rhythm in the history of American naturalism is confirmed by the principal biographical fact of the movement—that young men of great talent at three specific moments in American literary history have written long naturalistic novels but have gone on, at the end of these periods, to widely different individual interests. (Among major naturalists, perhaps only Dreiser violates this rule.)

American naturalists of the 1890s explored in a frequently muddled yet fundamental way the two interrelated concerns of American naturalism: the tragic nature of life because of the determining forces of experience, and the extent to which affirmative humanistic value and meaning could still be found despite man's conditioned life. These two concerns, the first more social, the second more abstractly philosophical, reappear in the decades of the 1930s and of the late 1940s and early 1950s. In particular, the naturalists of the late 1940s and early 1950s made even more explicit and clear the underlying dualism of the naturalism of the 1890s, a dualism in which the writer does not merely accept the reality of the conditioning forces of life but actively seeks belief and value within this reality.

The American naturalistic novel has not had a single dominant form or shape but rather several recurring forms among novels of different periods, a characteristic which suggests the existence of certain fundamental fictional responses to the naturalistic impulse. One such recurring form is the novel of group defeat, in which a powerful social or economic force causes the fall of a particular class or group of men, even though some individuals in this group are able to push through to a semi-mystical insight. In such novels as *The Octopus*, *The Grapes of Wrath*, and *The Naked and the Dead*, this is naturalism at its most epic and allegorical. Another continuing naturalistic form is the novel of questing, as in *The Red Badge of Courage*, *Sister Carrie* (for Carrie), and *The Adventures of Augie*

March, in which the protagonist seeks inconclusively in a shifting, ambivalent, and often destructive world some form of certainty about himself. A third kind of naturalistic novel records the fall and death of figures completely overwhelmed by the conditions of their lives, as in *Maggie, McTeague,* and *Lie Down in Darkness.* In these works a compensating factor is the element of tragic pathos in the undoing of weak figures who nevertheless, aside from the specific circumstances of their existence, have the capacity for some satisfaction in their experience. And a final form of naturalism dramatizes in massive detail the failure of American society to offer an adequate context for the development of the felt life, as in *An American Tragedy, Studs Lonigan,* and *U.S.A.*

It would be futile to attempt to predict the future of naturalism in America, or even if it has a future. One can perhaps point, as recent harbingers, to the fiction of Joyce Carol Oates and to the transfer of some of the interests and techniques of literary naturalism to such forms as the film (for example, *The Deer Hunter*) and documentary narrative (for example, *In Cold Blood*). But we must wait to see.

Notes

Bibliography

Index

Notes

Preface

1. *American Writing in the Twentieth Century* (Cambridge, Mass.: Harvard Univ. Pr., 1960), p. 180.
2. The best brief discussion of naturalism as a world-wide movement is by Lilian R. Furst and Peter N. Skrine, *Naturalism* (London: Methuen, 1971).
3. This is basically the view of George J. Becker in his influential "Introduction" to his edition of *Documents of Modern Literary Realism* (Princeton: Princeton Univ. Pr., 1963).
4. An unusually acute endorsement of this conventional notion occurs in Edwin H. Cady's essay "Three Sensibilities: Romancer, Realist, Naturalist" in his *The Light of Common Day: Realism in American Fiction* (Bloomington: Indiana Univ. Pr., 1971).
5. *American Literary Naturalism, A Divided Stream* (Minneapolis: Univ. of Minnesota Pr., 1956).
6. "'Not Men': A Natural History of American Naturalism," *Kenyon Review* 9 (Summer 1947): 414–35; reprinted in expanded form in *Documents*, ed. Becker, as "A Natural History of American Naturalism."
7. "American Naturalism: Reflections from Another Era," *New Mexico Quarterly* 20 (Spring 1950): 50.
8. "Zola as a Romantic Writer," San Francisco *Wave* 15 (June 27, 1896): 3; reprinted in *The Literary Criticism of Frank Norris*, ed. Donald Pizer (Austin: Univ. of Texas Pr., 1964), p. 72.
9. Richard Chase, *The American Novel and Its Tradition* (Garden City, N.Y.: Doubleday, 1957).
10. The standard histories of late nineteenth-century American literature contain full discussions of the movement in the 1890s. (See those listed on p. 156 n. 1.) In addition, extensive discussion of late nineteenth-century American naturalism occurs in Lars Ahnebrink, *The Beginnings of Naturalism in American Fiction . . . 1891–1903* (Cambridge, Mass.: Harvard Univ. Pr., 1950); Charles C. Walcutt, *American Literary Naturalism*; and *American Literary Naturalism: A Reassessment*, ed. Yoshinobu Hakutani and Lewis Fried (Heidelberg: Carl Winter, 1975).
11. See in particular my essays "Late Nineteenth-Century American Naturalism," in my *Realism and Naturalism in Nineteenth-Century American Literature* (Carbondale: Southern Illinois Univ. Pr., 1966); "Nineteenth-Century American Naturalism: An Approach Through Form," *Forum* (Houston), 13 (Winter 1976): 43–46; and "American Literary Naturalism: The Example of Dreiser," *Studies in American Fiction* 5 (Spring 1977): 51–64. The first two essays concentrate on *The Red Badge of Courage*, *McTeague*, and *Sister Carrie*. See also my *The Novels of Frank Norris* (Bloomington: Indiana Univ. Pr., 1966) and *The Novels of Theodore Dreiser: A Critical Study* (Minneapolis: Univ. of Minnesota Pr., 1976).

Introduction

1. See the standard literary histories of the period: Warner Berthoff, *The Ferment of Realism: American Literature, 1884–1919* (New York: Free Press, 1965); Jay Martin, *Harvests of Change: American Literature, 1865–1914* (Englewood Cliffs, N.J.: Prentice-Hall, 1967); and Larzer Ziff, *The American 1890s: Life and Times of a Lost Generation* (New York: Viking, 1966). My own *American Thought and Writing: The 1890s* (Boston: Houghton Mifflin, 1972) is an interpretive anthology of the decade.
2. *Stephen Crane: Letters*, ed. R. W. Stallman and Lillian Gilkes (New York: New York Univ. Pr., 1960), p. 14.
3. *The Red Badge of Courage*, ed. Donald Pizer (New York: Norton, Norton Critical Edition, 2nd ed., 1976), p. 21.
4. *Sister Carrie*, ed. Donald Pizer (New York: Norton, Norton Critical Edition, 1970), p. 56.
5. See Lars Ahnebrink, *The Beginnings of Naturalism in American Fiction . . . 1891–1903* (Cambridge, Mass.: Harvard Univ. Pr., 1950) for Zola's impact on the young American writers of the 1890s.
6. I refer to Jimmie's awe at the beauty of the moon and Maggie's display of the lambrequin for Pete. (Maggie purchases the lambrequin out of an unconscious sense that beauty is associated with love and that beauty must therefore be made visible if love is to be known.) I discuss the theme of beauty in *Maggie* in my introduction to a facsimile edition of the 1893 *Maggie* (San Francisco: Chandler, 1968).
7. See Frederick J. Hoffman's important posthumous essay, "From Document to Symbol: Zola and American Naturalism," *Revue des Langues Vivantes*, U.S. Bicentennial Issue (1976), pp. 203–12.

Preface: The 1930s

1. There is no book-length study of American naturalism in the 1930s, though discussion of individual writers as naturalists occurs in Alfred Kazin, *On Native Grounds* (New York: Reynal & Hitchcock, 1942); Charles C. Walcutt, *American Literary Naturalism, A Divided Stream* (Minneapolis: Univ. of Minnesota Pr., 1956); Willard Thorp, *American Writing in the Twentieth Century* (Cambridge, Mass.: Harvard Univ. Pr., 1960); and *American Literary Naturalism: A Reassessment*, ed. Yoshinobu Hakutani and Lewis Fried (Heidelberg: Carl Winter, 1975).
2. Richard H. Pells, *Radical Visions and American Dreams: Culture and Social Thought in the Depression Years* (New York: Harper & Row, 1973).
3. "James T. Farrell," *Talks with Authors*, ed. Charles F. Madden (Carbondale: Southern Illinois Univ. Pr., 1968), p. 96.

James T. Farrell: Studs Lonigan

1. Edgar M. Branch, *James T. Farrell* (New York: Twayne, 1971), pp. 36–37. I am

indebted to Branch's excellent study for other biographical details about Farrell which appear in this chapter.

2. Barry Wallenstein discusses this and other stereotyped approaches to Farrell's work in his "James T. Farrell: Critic of Naturalism," in *American Literary Naturalism: A Reassessment*, ed. Yoshinobu Hakutani and Lewis Fried (Heidelberg: Carl Winter, 1975), pp. 154–57.

3. "Introduction," *Studs Lonigan* (New York: Modern Library, 1938), p. x.

4. See, in particular, Farrell's comments in "The Author as Plaintiff: Testimony in a Censorship Case," *Reflections at Fifty and Other Essays* (London: Neville Spearman, 1956 [1954]), pp. 188–223.

5. *Studs Lonigan*, pp. xi, xii, xiv.

6. "The Author as Plaintiff," p. 191. See also Farrell's comment in *Conversations with Writers, II* (Detroit: Gale, 1978), p. 28, that *Studs* is "a psychological novel. Much of the world as presented in *Studs Lonigan* is presented through Studs' consciousness."

7. *A Note on Literary Criticism* (New York: Vanguard, 1936), p. 98. Farrell's most detailed later account of the influence of Joyce upon him during his early career occurs in his 1977 interview with Matthew J. Bruccoli in *Conversations with Writers, II*, pp. 23–24.

8. *Gas-House McGinty* (Cleveland: World, 1943 [1933]), p. 38.

9. See Farrell's undated letter to Victor Weybright, quoted by Branch, *James T. Farrell*, p. 173 n. 1, and *Conversations with Writers, II*, pp. 23–24. As Farrell noted in his letter, he used in *Judgment Day* only a small portion of the lengthy deathbed fantasy which he wrote for the novel.

10. "A Note on Sherwood Anderson," *Reflections at Fifty*, pp. 164–66.

11. For this aspect of Farrell's thought, see Branch's *James T. Farrell* (which incorporates earlier essays by him on the subject) and Lewis Fried, "James T. Farrell: Shadow and Act," *Jahrbuch für Amerikastudien* 17 (Apr. 1972): 140–55.

12. *Studs Lonigan* (New York: Modern Library, 1938), *Young Lonigan*, p. 3. Citations from *Studs Lonigan* are from this edition and will hereafter appear in the text. Since the novels of *Studs Lonigan* are separately paginated in this edition, I will cite both the novel and the page number, using the following abbreviations: YL—*Young Lonigan*; YM—*The Young Manhood of Studs Lonigan*; JD—*Judgment Day*.

13. See Robert Humphrey, *Stream of Consciousness in the Modern Novel* (Berkeley: Univ. of California Pr., 1954) and Melvin Friedman, *Stream of Consciousness: A Study in Literary Method* (New Haven: Yale Univ. Pr., 1955).

14. *The Dual Voice: Free Indirect Speech and Its Functioning in the Nineteenth-Century European Novel* (Manchester: Manchester Univ. Pr., 1977).

15. *The Dual Voice*, p. 137.

16. For Farrell's use of "free association" in connection with *Studs Lonigan*, see "An In-Depth Interview with James T. Farrell," *Writer's Forum* 1 (May 1965): 34, and "James T. Farrell," in *Talks with Authors*, ed. Charles F. Madden (Carbondale: Southern Illinois Univ. Pr., 1968), p. 97. For his use of "stream of consciousness," see his 1935 essay, "Farrell's Introduction to Chilean Edition of 'Young Lonigan,'" *American Book Collector* 17 (May 1967): 8. One of the few efforts to discuss *Studs* as a stream-of-consciousness novel is Ann Douglas's "*Studs Lonigan* and the Failure of History in Mass Society," *American Quarterly* 29 (Winter 1977): 487–505.

17. See also *The Young Manhood of Studs Lonigan*, p. 132.

18. See also *Judgment Day*, p. 244.

John Dos Passos: U.S.A.

1. The principal works by Dos Passos which provide information about his life and ideas are *The Best Times: An Informal Memoir* (New York: New American Library, 1966); *Occasions and Protests* (Chicago: Henry Regnery, 1964), a collection of essays; and *The Fourteenth Chronicle: Letters and Diaries of John Dos Passos*, ed. Townsend Ludington (Boston: Gambit, 1973).

2. Some influential early studies which stress these themes in Dos Passos' work are: Maxwell Geismar, *Writers in Crisis: The American Novel, 1925–1940* (Boston: Houghton Mifflin, 1942), pp. 87–139; Alfred Kazin, *On Native Grounds* (New York: Reynal & Hitchcock, 1942) pp. 341–59; and Malcolm Cowley, "The Poet and the World," *New Republic* 70 (Apr. 27, 1932): 303–5. (The essays by Kazin and Cowley are reprinted in *Dos Passos, the Critics, and the Writer's Intention*, ed. Allen Belkind [Carbondale: Southern Illinois Univ. Pr., 1971]). The themes appear in Dos Passos' essays as early as "A Humble Protest," *Harvard Monthly* 62 (June 1916): 115–20, and "America and the Pursuit of Happiness," *Nation* 160 (Dec. 29, 1920): 777–78.

3. *The Fourteenth Chronicle*, p. 193.

4. The fullest study of Dos Passos' debt to his father's ideas occurs in Melvin Landsberg's *Dos Passos' Path to "U.S.A.": A Political Biography, 1912–1936* (Boulder: Colorado Associated Univ. Pr., 1972), pp. 1–19. See also Dos Passos' own account in *The Best Times*, pp. 1–40.

5. See Landsberg, *Dos Passos' Path to "U.S.A.,"* for a number of other such borrowings by Dos Passos.

6. "Looking Back on U.S.A.," *New York Times*, Oct. 25, 1959, sec. 2, p. 5.

7. "Statement of Belief," *Bookman* 68 (Sept. 1928): 26.

8. Introduction, *Three Soldiers* (New York: Modern Library, 1932), p. vii.

9. *U.S.A.* (New York: Modern Library, 1937), p. vii. Citations will hereafter appear in the text. Since the three novels of *U.S.A* are paginated separately in this edition, I will cite both the novel and the page numbers, using the following abbreviations: FP—*The 42nd Parallel*; NN—*Nineteen Nineteen*; and BM—*The Big Money*.

10. Joseph Warren Beach offers some shrewd early comments on Dos Passos' verbal irony in his *American Fiction, 1920–1940* (New York: Macmillan, 1941), p. 66. A more recent discussion is by David L. Vanderwerken, *"U.S.A.:* Dos Passos and the 'Old Words,'" *Twentieth Century Literature* 23 (May 1977): 195–228.

11. Landsberg, *Dos Passos' Path to "U.S.A.,"* p. 254 n. 41. A number of critics have commented in passing on the relationship between Dos Passos' narrative prose style in *U.S.A.* and Joycean stream of consciousness. These include John Lydenberg, "Dos Passos's *U.S.A.:* The Words of the Hollow Men," in *Essays on Determinism in American Literature*, ed. Sydney J. Krause (Kent, Ohio: Kent State Univ. Pr., 1964), pp. 97–107; Herbert M. McLuhan, "John Dos Passos: Technique vs. Sensibility," in *Dos Passos: A Collection of Critical Essays*, ed. Andrew Hook, (Englewood Cliffs, N.J.: Prentice-Hall, 1974), 148–61; George J. Becker, *John Dos Passos* (New

York: Frederick Ungar, 1974), p. 48. One of the earliest comments about stream of consciousness in Dos Passos' fiction occurs in Jean-Paul Sartre's "John Dos Passos and *1919*" (1947), in *Dos Passos*, ed. Hook, pp. 61–69.

12. *U.S.A.*, p. vii.

13. "The Search for Identity in the Novels of John Dos Passos," *PMLA* 76 (Mar. 1961): 133–49; quoted from *Dos Passos*, ed. Belkind, p. 187.

14. Frank Gado, "An Interview with John Dos Passos," *Idol: The Literary Quarterly of Union College* 45 (1969): 23.

15. A brief discussion of this aspect of the Camera Eye occurs in Townsend Ludington's "The Ordering of the Camera Eye in *U.S.A.*," *American Literature* 49 (Nov. 1977): 443–46.

16. *Writers on the Left* (New York, 1961), p. 348. Landsberg, in his *Dos Passos' Path to "U.S.A.*," has a full account of Dos Passos' political ideas of the 1920s and 1930s. He and others have noted the important role which Dos Passos' dismay over the Communist involvement in the Harlan mine workers' strike played in his growing antagonism to the party.

John Steinbeck: The Grapes of Wrath

1. Two collections of Steinbeck criticism contain most of the pertinent commentary on *The Grapes of Wrath: A Casebook on "The Grapes of Wrath*," ed. Agnes McNeill Donohue (New York: Crowell, 1968) and *Steinbeck: A Collection of Critical Essays*, ed. Robert M. Davis (Englewood Cliffs, N.J.: Prentice-Hall, 1972). The two most important views of Steinbeck as a naturalist are Woodburn O. Ross, "John Steinbeck: Naturalism's Priest," *College English* 10 (May 1949): 432–38 and Warren French, "John Steinbeck: A Usable Concept of Naturalism," in *American Literary Naturalism: A Reassessment*, ed. Yoshinobu Hakutani and Lewis Fried (Heidelberg: Carl Winter, 1975), pp. 122–35 (also in French's second edition of his *John Steinbeck* [New York: Twayne, 1975]). Ross stresses the mysticism at the center of Steinbeck's naturalism, and French views *The Grapes of Wrath* as a move by Steinbeck from naturalism to a "drama of consciousness." My "John Steinbeck and American Naturalism," *Steinbeck Quarterly* 9 (Winter 1976): 12–15, concentrates on *Of Mice and Men*.

2. In the absence of a full-scale biography, Peter Lisca's *The Wide World of John Steinbeck* (New Brunswick, N.J.: Rutgers Univ. Pr., 1958) and Elaine Steinbeck's and Robert Wallsten's *Steinbeck: A Life in Letters* (New York: Viking, 1975), are the best sources for information about Steinbeck's life.

3. See Jackson J. Benson, "'To Tom, Who Lived It': John Steinbeck and the Man from Weedpatch," *Journal of Modern Literature* 5 (Apr. 1976), 151–94.

4. "A Primer on the 30's," *Esquire* 53 (June 1960): 85–93.

5. "John Steinbeck: The Boys in the Back Room," *Classics and Commercials* (New York: Farrar, Straus, 1950), p. 44.

6. Wilson, *Classics*, p. 36, and J. Paul Hunter, "Steinbeck's Wine of Affirmation in *The Grapes of Wrath*," in *Essays in Modern American Literature*, ed. Richard E. Langford (DeLand, Fla.: Stetson Univ. Pr., 1963), pp. 76–89.

7. *Sea of Cortez* was initially published in 1941. A useful later edition is Steinbeck's

The Log from the Sea of Cortez: The Narrative Portion of the Book "Sea of Cortez" with a Profile "About Ed Ricketts" (London: Heineman, 1958 [1951]). The "Easter Sunday" chapter in the *Log* is pp. 131–51.

8. *The Log from the Sea of Cortez*, p. 165.

9. *Steinbeck: A Life in Letters*, p. 76. See also pp. 81 and 87.

10. As early as 1948 Frederick Bracher, in his "Steinbeck and the Biological View of Man," *Pacific Spectator* 2 (Winter 1948): 14–29, announced that Steinbeck had derived the non-teleological thinking passage in *Sea of Cortez* from Ricketts' journals. Not until the appearance of Astro's study in 1973, however, was Ricketts' responsibility for the passage fully substantiated. Nevertheless, some critics—for example, Jackson J. Benson, in his "John Steinbeck: Novelist as Scientist," *Novel* 10 (Spring 1977): 248–64—continue to attempt to reconcile the ideas of the passage with Steinbeck's ideas in his fiction.

11. *The Log from the Sea of Cortez*, pp. 247–50.

12. *The Grapes of Wrath* (New York: Viking, 1939), p. 32. Citations will hereafter appear in the text.

13. Steinbeck first uses the "I" to "We" formulation on pp. 206–7, soon after the Joads begin their journey to California.

14. In perhaps a conscious effort to make a connection between the Wilsons and other such families later in the novel—the Wallaces at Weedpatch and the Wainwrights in the boxcar—Steinbeck begins all three surnames with the same letter.

15. *The Octopus*, in *Collected Writings of Frank Norris* (Garden City, N.Y.: Doubleday, Doran, 1928), vol. 2, p. 361.

Preface: The Late 1940s and early 1950s

1. "Notes on the Decline of Naturalism," *Partisan Review* 9 (Nov.-Dec. 1942), 483–93, reprinted in Philip Rahv's *Image and Idea* (New York: New Directions, 1949) and in *Documents of Modern Literary Realism*, ed. George J. Becker (Princeton: Princeton Univ. Pr., 1963), p. 589.

2. Trilling, "Reality in America," *The Liberal Imagination* (Garden City, N.Y.: Doubleday, 1957 [1950]), pp. 1–19 (Trilling's essay appeared initially in two parts in 1940 and 1946); Cowley, "'Not Men': A Natural History of American Naturalism," *Kenyon Review* 9 (Summer 1947), 414–35, reprinted in *Documents*, ed. Becker, pp. 429–51.

3. *American Writing in the Twentieth Century* (Cambridge, Mass.: Harvard Univ. Pr., 1960), p. 144.

4. Bellow was born in 1915, Mailer in 1923, and Styron in 1925.

5. *Advertisements for Myself* (New York: Putnam, 1959), p. 27.

6. See Mailer's "Modes and Mutations: Quick Comments on the Modern American Novel," *Commentary* 41 (Mar. 1966): 37–40, reprinted in Mailer's *Cannibals and Christians* (New York: Dial, 1966), pp. 95–103, and Bellow's "Starting Out in Chicago," *American Scholar* 44 (Winter 1974/75): 73. Mailer in his essay does not specifically state his indebtedness to Dreiser, but such an indebtedness for *The Naked and the Dead* can be inferred from his laudatory discussion of Dreiser's social realism.

7. The first two quoted phrases are by Richard Lehan in his *A Dangerous Crossing: French Literary Existentialism and the Modern American Novel* (Carbondale: Southern Illinois Univ. Pr., 1973), p. xix; the last is by David D. Galloway in his *The Absurd Hero in American Fiction* (Austin: Univ. of Texas Pr., 1966), p. x.

Norman Mailer: The Naked and the Dead

1. A number of essays reflecting these views can be found in two of the major collections of Mailer criticism: *Norman Mailer: The Man and His Work*, ed. Robert F. Lucid (Boston: Little, Brown, 1971) and *Norman Mailer: A Collection of Critical Essays*, ed. Leo Braudy (Englewood Cliffs, N.J.: Prentice-Hall 1972). Perhaps the fullest account of Mailer as a 1930s novelist in *The Naked and the Dead* occurs in Chester E. Eisinger's *Fiction of the Forties* (Chicago: Univ. of Chicago Pr., 1963), pp. 33–38. In his *Norman Mailer: The Radical as Hipster* (Metuchen, N.J.: Scarecrow, 1978), Robert Ehrlich discusses the novel almost entirely as a foreshadowing of Mailer's later ideas. Superior general critiques of *The Naked and the Dead* can be found in Robert Solotaroff's *Down Mailer's Way* (Urbana: Univ. of Illinois Pr., 1974); Jean Radford's *Norman Mailer: A Critical Study* (New York: Barnes & Noble, 1975); and Robert Merrill's *Norman Mailer* (New York; Twayne, 1978).

2. *Advertisements for Myself* (New York: Putnam, 1959), p. 27.

3. *The Literary Situation* (New York: Viking, 1954), p. 36.

4. *The Naked and the Dead* (New York: Rinehart, 1948), p. 324. Citations will hereafter appear in the text.

5. Louise Levitas, "*The naked* are fanatics *and the dead* don't care," *New York Star* (Magazine Section), Aug. 22, 1948, p. 3.

6. The essay is republished in Mailer's *Advertisements for Myself*.

7. Podhoretz's essay appeared originally in *Partisan Review*; it is reprinted in his *Doings and Undoings* (New York: Farrar, Straus, 1964), and in *Norman Mailer*, ed. Lucid.

8. Paul Krassner, "An Impolite Interview," *The Realist* (Dec. 1962), reprinted in Mailer's *The Presidential Papers* (New York: Berkley, 1970 [1963]), p. 136.

9. Levitas, "The naked," p. 4.

10. Harvey Breit, "A Talk with Norman Mailer," *New York Times*, June 3, 1951; reprinted in Breit's *The Writer Observed* (Cleveland: World, 1956), p. 200.

11. I agree, however, with John M. Muste's contention, in his "Norman Mailer and John Dos Passos: The Question of Influence," *Modern Fiction Studies* 17 (Autumn 1971): 361–74, that Dos Passos' *Three Soldiers* has been neglected as a possible major influence on *The Naked and the Dead*. Dos Passos' pervasive machine symbolism and his characterization of John Andrews as an intellectual who makes a tragic gesture toward human freedom have clear parallels in Mailer's novel.

12. Breit, *The Writer Observed*, pp. 199–200. Two useful discussions of the relationship between *Moby Dick* and *The Naked and the Dead* are Michael Cowan, "The Americanness of Norman Mailer," in *Norman Mailer*, ed. Braudy, and Edward Stone, "*Moby Dick* and Mailer's *Naked and the Dead*," *Extracts* 30 (1977): 15–17.

13. "Some Children of the Goddess," *Esquire* 60 (July 1963); reprinted in Mailer's *Cannibals and Christians* (New York: Dial, 1966), p. 128.

14. Mailer commented in his essay, "Modes and Mutations: Quick Comments on the Modern American Novel," *Commentary* 41 (Mar. 1966): 38, that Dreiser "came closer to understanding the social machine than any American writer."

15. "Norman Mailer," *Current Biography: 1948* (New York: H. W. Wilson, 1948), p. 410.

16. Levitas, *"The naked,"* p. 4.

17. *Thus Spake Zarathustra* (New York: Modern Library, 1917), pp. 27–29.

18. Mailer was later to make the relationship between sex and power one of his principal fictional themes. Like Mailer, Henry Miller grew up in Brooklyn, a milieu, Mailer commented, which "was incapable of experiencing sex without the power relation of sex"—*Genius and Lust: A Journey Through the Major Writings of Henry Miller*, ed. Norman Mailer (New York: Bantam, 1977), p. 151.

19. The statement is actually Hearn's summing up, in question form, of a long speech by Cummings. Cummings' reply to the question is "Yes."

20. For Cummings, see p. 300; for Croft, see p. 532.

21. *Literature and Dogma* (1873), in *The Works of Matthew Arnold* (London: Macmillan, 1903), vol. 7, p. 41.

22. See, for example, Solotaroff, *Down Mailer's Way*, pp. 35–39.

23. "Rugged Times," *New Yorker* 24 (Oct. 23, 1948): 25.

24. Levitas, *"The naked,"* p. 4.

25. Goldstein's allusion to "gas chambers" appears to be an anachronism. There was little general awareness of Nazi extermination camps until after the war.

26. The more infrequent "Choruses"—brief scenes of stylized dialogue dealing with archetypal moments and concerns of the enlisted man—are less derivative. One of them, "Rotation," is very similar in theme to Joseph Heller's *Catch–22*: "That rotation ain't a plan to get men home, it's a plan how not to get them home" (500).

27. Breit, *The Writer Observed*, p. 201.

William Styron: Lie Down in Darkness

1. For this aspect of *Lie Down in Darkness*, see in particular Melvin J. Friedman, "William Styron: An Interim Appraisal," *English Journal* 50 (Mar. 1961): 149–58, 192; Marvin Klotz, "The Triumph over Time: Narrative Form in William Faulkner and William Styron," *Mississippi Quarterly* 17 (Winter 1963/64): 9–20; and Louis D. Rubin, "Notes on a Southern Writer in Our Time," *The Faraway Country* (Seattle: Univ. of Washington Pr., 1963), reprinted in *The Achievement of William Styron*, ed. Robert K. Morris and Irving Malin (Athens: Univ. of Georgia Pr., 1975), pp. 51–87.

2. See Harriet Doar, "Interview with William Styron," *Red Clay Reader* 1 (1964): 28.

3. David Dempsey, "Talk with William Styron," *New York Times Book Review*, September 9, 1951, p. 27.

4. Peter Matthiessen and George Plimpton, "William Styron," *Writers at Work: The "Paris Review" Interviews*, ed. Malcolm Cowley (New York: Viking, 1959), p. 272.

5. David L. Stevenson, "Styron and the Fiction of the Fifties," *Critique* 3 (Summer 1960): 48, 49. David D. Galloway also discusses *Lie Down in Darkness* as an example

of a native American existentialism in *The Absurd Hero in American Fiction* (Austin: Univ. of Texas Pr., 1966).

6. Styron's phrase, in the context of his discussion of tragic art, from his preface to *Under Twenty-Five: Duke Narrative and Verse, 1945–1962*, ed. William Blackburn (Durham, N.C.: Duke Univ. Pr., 1963), p. 7.

7. *Lie Down in Darkness* (New York: Viking, 1951), p. 374. Citations will hereafter appear in the text.

8. "Zola as a Romantic Writer," in *The Literary Criticism of Frank Norris*, ed. Donald Pizer (Austin: Univ. of Texas Pr., 1964), p. 72.

9. Frederick J. Hoffman also makes this point in his excellent "William Styron: The Metaphysical Hurt," *The Art of Southern Fiction* (Carbondale: Southern Illinois Univ. Pr., 1967), p. 151.

10. For a typical discussion, see Marc L. Ratner, *William Styron* (New York: Twayne, 1972), pp. 54–56.

11. *American Moderns: From Rebellion to Conformity* (New York: Hill and Wang, 1958), p. 242.

12. Styron heightens still further the importance of the ferry and train in the symbolic structure of the novel by enclosing the two double journeys within a frame involving them. The novel opens with a brief section in which the reader (a "you" from the North) is introduced to Port Warwick as he arrives from Richmond by train, with the train journey ending at the station dock. The novel concludes with a train leaving Port Warwick for Richmond.

13. Milton repeats this statement verbatim on p. 103.

14. Jack Griffin, "A Conversation with William Styron," *Pennsylvania Review* 1 (Spring 1967): 26. The interview occurred in January 1965.

15. Griffin, "A Conversation," p. 29.

16. "William Styron," p. 149.

Saul Bellow: The Adventures of Augie March

1. See Bellow's own comment on *The Victim* in his 1965 *Paris Review* interview in *Writers at Work: The "Paris Review" Interviews, Third Series*, ed. George Plimpton (New York: Penguin, 1977 [1967]), p. 187.

2. Harvey Breit, "Saul Bellow," *The Writer Observed* (Cleveland: World, 1956), p. 273. The interview occurred in 1953.

3. The phrase is James H. Justus's in his review of Bellow criticism for 1976 in *American Literary Scholarship: An Annual/1976*, ed. J. Albert Robbins (Durham, N.C.: Duke Univ. Pr., 1978), p. 297.

4. Some other discussions of *Augie* as a naturalistic novel are: Kingsley Widmer, "Poetic Naturalism in the Contemporary Novel," *Partisan Review* 26 (Summer 1959): 467–72; Richard Chase, "The Adventures of Saul Bellow," *Commentary* 27 (April 1959), 223–30, reprinted in *Saul Bellow and the Critics*, ed. Irving Malin (New York: New York Univ. Pr., 1967), pp. 25–38; Malcolm Bradbury, "Saul Bellow and the Naturalist Tradition," *Review of English Literature* 4 (Oct. 1963): 80–92; and Earl Rovit, "Saul Bellow and Norman Mailer: The Secret Sharers," in *Saul Bellow: A Collection of Critical Essays*, ed. Earl Rovit (Englewood Cliffs, N.J.:

Prentice-Hall, 1975), pp. 161–70. Among other essays on *Augie*, I have profited in particular from Albert J. Guerard's "Saul Bellow and the Activists," *Southern Review* 3 (Summer 1967): 582–96.

5. *The Adventures of Augie March* (New York: Viking, 1953), p. 536. Citations will hereafter appear in the text.

6. Sanford Pinsker, "Saul Bellow in the Classroom," *College English* 34 (Apr. 1973): 976.

7. John Enck, "Saul Bellow: An Interview," *Wisconsin Studies in Contemporary Litera-ture* 6 (Summer 1965): 156–57

8. The phrase occurs in Bellow's "The Writer as Moralist," *Atlantic Monthly* 211 (Mar. 1963): 60, where Bellow writes, "If a novelist is going to affirm anything, he must be prepared to prove his case in close detail, reconcile it with hard facts."

9. See Bellow's "Starting Out in Chicago," *American Scholar* 44 (Winter 1974/75): 73.

10. As has been frequently noted, Bellow's working title for *Augie March* was "Life Among the Machiavellians."

11. *City of Words: American Fiction, 1950–1970* (New York: Harper & Row, 1971), p. 71.

12. Bellow on several occasions has expressed his contempt for the Lawrence of *The Plumed Serpent*. See his "Where Do We Go from Here: The Future of Fiction" (1962), in *Saul Bellow and the Critics*, ed. Malin. p. 212, and his *Paris Review* interview (1965), p. 182.

13. Augie also encounters a number of other "theoreticians"—Manny Padilla, Clem Tambow, and Robey—who are scientists manqué and who seek to enlist him in their visions of truth. But since he is neither in love with these figures nor confined in a boat with them, he is more readily able to dismiss their threat to his freedom.

14. Sylvester (along with Mimi's lover Frazer) also plays a role in the satire of 1930s radical politics which runs through *Augie March*. Both are expelled from the Communist Party for "Infantile Leftism and Trotskyist Deviationism" (p. 212) and Frazer ultimately becomes a major in U.S. Army Intelligence.

15. "The Sealed Treasure," *Times Literary Supplement*, July 1, 1960, p. 414. See also Bellow's 1965 statement that "I seem to have asked in my books, How can one resist the controls of this vast society *without* turning into a nihilist, avoiding the absurdity of empty rebellion?" (*Paris Review* interview, p. 196).

16. On his return from Mexico City, Augie discovers human parallels to the flower and kinkajou in his brother George and his mother. George is mentally defective and his mother blind. Besides being imprisoned by their defects, both are also encaged in "homes." Yet both accept their fate with dignity, Augie decides, and thus embellish it. (See pp. 419–21).

Bibliography

Works About American Literary Naturalism

Ahnebrink, Lars. *The Beginnings of Naturalism in American Fiction . . . 1891–1903*. Cambridge, Mass.: Harvard Univ. Pr., 1950.

Becker, George J. "Introduction: Modern Realism as a Literary Movement," *Documents of Modern Literary Realism*, ed. George J. Becker. Princeton: Princeton Univ. Pr., 1963.

Block, Haskell M., "Introduction: The Problem of Naturalism," *Naturalistic Triptych*. New York: Random House, 1970.

Bowron, Bernard R., Jr. "Realism in America," *Comparative Literature* 3 (Summer 1951): 268–85.

Budd, Louis J. "Objectivity and Low Seriousness in American Naturalism," *Prospects* 1 (1975): 41–61.

Cady, Edwin H. "Three Sensibilities: Romancer, Realist, Naturalist," *The Light of Common Day: Realism in American Fiction*. Bloomington: Indiana Univ. Pr., 1971.

Cowley, Malcolm. "'Not Men': A Natural History of American Naturalism," *Kenyon Review* 9 (Summer 1947): 414–35.

Farrell, James T. "Some Observations on Naturalism, So Called, in Fiction," *Reflections at Fifty and Other Essays*. New York: Vanguard, 1954.

Figg, Robert M., III. "Naturalism as a Literary Form," *Georgia Review* 18 (Fall 1964): 308–16.

Furst, Lilian R., and Skrine, Peter N. *Naturalism*. London: Methuen, 1971.

Hakutani, Yoshinobu. "Introduction," *American Literary Naturalism: A Reassessment*, ed. Yoshinobu Hakutani and Lewis Fried. Heidelberg: Carl Winter, 1975.

Hoffman, Frederick J. "From Document to Symbol: Zola and American Naturalism," *Revue des Langues Vivantes*, U.S. Bicentennial Issue (1976), pp. 203–12.

Kazin, Alfred. "American Naturalism: Reflections from Another Era," *The American Writer and the European Tradition*, ed. Margaret Denny and William H. Gilman. Minneapolis: Univ. of Minnesota Pr., 1950.

Pizer, Donald. "Late Nineteenth-Century American Naturalism," *Realism and Naturalism in Nineteenth-Century American Literature*. Carbondale: Southern Illinois Univ. Pr., 1966.

———. "Nineteenth-Century American Naturalism: An Approach Through Form," *Forum* (Houston), 13 (Winter 1976): 43–46.

———. "American Literary Naturalism: The Example of Dreiser," *Studies in American Fiction* 5 (Spring 1977): 51–63.

Rahv, Philip. "Notes on the Decline of Naturalism," *Image and Idea*. New York: New Directions, 1949.

Thorp, Willard. "The Persistence of Naturalism in the Novel," *American Writing in the Twentieth Century.* Cambridge, Mass.: Harvard Univ. Pr., 1960.

Walcutt, Charles C. *American Literary Naturalism, A Divided Stream.* Minneapolis: Univ. of Minnesota Pr., 1956.

Major Studies of James T. Farrell, John Dos Passos, John Steinbeck, Norman Mailer, William Styron, and Saul Bellow

Aaron, Daniel. *Writers on the Left.* New York: Harcourt, Brace, and World, 1961. (Farrell and Dos Passos)

Astro, Richard. *John Steinbeck and Edward F. Ricketts: The Shaping of a Novelist.* Minneapolis: Univ. of Minnesota Pr., 1973.

Beach, Joseph Warren. *American Fiction, 1920–1940.* New York: Macmillan, 1941. (Farrell, Dos Passos, and Steinbeck)

Belkind, Allen, ed. *Dos Passos, the Critics, and the Writer's Intention.* Carbondale: Southern Illinois Univ. Pr., 1971.

Branch, Edgar M. *James T. Farrell.* New York: Twayne, 1971.

Braudy, Leo, ed. *Norman Mailer: A Collection of Critical Essays.* Englewood Cliffs, N.J.: Prentice-Hall, 1972.

Colley, Iain. *Dos Passos and the Fiction of Despair.* Totowa, N.J.: Rowman and Littlefield, 1978.

Davis, Robert M., ed. *Steinbeck: A Collection of Critical Essays.* Englewood Cliffs, N.J.: Prentice-Hall, 1972.

Eisinger, Chester E. *Fiction of the Forties.* Chicago: Univ. of Chicago Pr., 1963. (Mailer and Bellow)

French, Warren. *John Steinbeck.* 2nd ed. New York: Twayne, 1975.

Frohock, Wilbur M. *The Novel of Violence in America.* 2nd ed. Dallas: Southern Methodist Univ. Pr., 1957. (Farrell, Dos Passos, and Steinbeck)

Galloway, David D. *The Absurd Hero in American Fiction.* 2nd ed. Austin: Univ. of Texas Pr., 1970. (Styron and Bellow)

Gelfant, Blanche H. *The American City Novel.* Norman: Univ. of Oklahoma Pr., 1954. (Farrell and Dos Passos)

Hassan, Ihab. *Radical Innocence, Studies in the Contemporary American Novel.* Princeton: Princeton Univ. Pr., 1961. (Mailer, Styron, and Bellow)

Hook, Andrew, ed. *Dos Passos: A Collection of Critical Essays.* Englewood Cliffs, N.J.: Prentice-Hall, 1974.

Kazin, Alfred. *On Native Grounds.* New York: Reynal and Hitchcock, 1942. (Farrell, Dos Passos, and Steinbeck)

Landsberg, Melvin. *Dos Passos' Path to "U.S.A.": A Political Biography.* Boulder: Colorado Associated Univ. Pr., 1972.

Lehan, Richard. *A Dangerous Crossing: French Literary Existentialism and the Modern American Novel.* Carbondale: Southern Illinois Univ. Pr., 1973. (Mailer and Bellow)

Levant, Howard. *The Novels of John Steinbeck: A Critical Study.* Columbia: Univ. of Missouri Pr., 1974.

Lisca, Peter. *The Wide World of John Steinbeck.* New Brunswick, N.J.: Rutgers Univ. Pr., 1958.

Lucid, Robert F., ed. *Norman Mailer: The Man and His Work.* Boston: Little, Brown, 1971.

Malin, Irving, ed. *Saul Bellow and the Critics.* New York: New York Univ. Pr., 1967.

Merrill, Robert. *Norman Mailer.* Boston: Twayne, 1978.

Morris, Robert K., and Malin, Irving, eds. *The Achievement of William Styron.* Athens: Univ. of Georgia Pr., 1975.

Radford Jean. *Norman Mailer: A Critical Study.* New York: Barnes & Noble, 1975.

Ratner, Marc L. *William Styron.* New York: Twayne, 1972.

Rovit, Earl, ed. *Saul Bellow: A Collection of Critical Essays.* Englewood Cliffs, N.J.: Prentice-Hall, 1975.

Solotaroff, Robert. *Down Mailer's Way.* Urbana: Univ. of Illinois Pr., 1974.

Tanner, Tony. *City of Words: American Fiction, 1950–70.* New York: Harper & Row, 1971. (Mailer and Bellow)

Wagner, Linda W. *Dos Passos: Artist as American.* Austin: Univ. of Texas Pr., 1979.

Index